"For those who have wondered  d a
spirituality and theological refl
clear, compelling, and practica
into the theological reflection p
several models of reflection-on
approach contemplation guides
ongoing conversion of the minister and confirms theological reflection
as a transformative process not only for the minister but also for the
ministry performed. The extensive use of personal experiences from
those she has worked with, especially members of Romero House in
Toronto, gives concreteness and appeal to the model she has developed."

—Robert L. Kinast
Center for Theological Reflection

"McAlpin's *Ministry That Transforms* marks a new more practical and more
spiritual stage in theological reflection. This book—clear, practical, and
forceful—makes explicit the requirements for graceful pastoral reflection
in today's world: a reflection firmly rooted in a community of faith and
action, where there exists an ongoing courtship of mercy and justice, with
the expectation of transformation—both of participants and the world. The
community of McAlpin's reflection is Romero House in Toronto, which
shelters immigrants and refugees as they arrive in Canada; here a ministry
of mercy flowers into demands of justice for society's most vulnerable
members. This model of contemplation in action would delight the heart
of Ignatius Loyola. Readers will find in McAlpin's two brief appendices an
excellent illustration of how her method of reflection proceeds. Few plea-
sures rival that of professors watching their student surpass them in a creative contribution to society."

—James and Evelyn Whitehead
Authors of *Method in Ministry*

"The powerful and convincing thesis of Kathleen McAlpin—that it is in the service of others and through reflection on that experience we become truly contemplative and authentic disciples of Jesus—is carefully and theologically articulated in this splendid book, *Ministry That Transforms*. Theories of transformational learning described by the author are brought to life through the experience of seven participants who the author comes to know as they assist refugees of Romero House through the legal procedures required to become landed immigrants in Canada. Particularly meaningful for me was the personal reflection of the author herself as she struggled and learned not to project her own perspectives and spirituality on the participants. This book offers not only content but above all reflection on an experience rooted in a compelling reality. It is a valuable tool for practitioners on many levels."

—Margaret Brennan, IHM
Professor Emerita
Regis College
Toronto, Ontario

Ministry That Transforms

A Contemplative Process
of Theological Reflection

Kathleen McAlpin

Foreword by Mary Jo Leddy

LITURGICAL PRESS
Collegeville, Minnesota

www.litpress.org

Cover design by Ann Blattner

1   2   3   4   5   6   7   8   9

Library of Congress Cataloging-in-Publication Data

McAlpin, Kathleen.
    Ministry that transforms : a contemplative process of theological
reflection / Kathleen McAlpin ; foreword by Mary Jo Leddy.
       p. cm.
    Includes bibliographical references and index.
    ISBN 978-0-8146-3222-2
    1. Church work.   2. Spirituality.   3. Conversion.   4. Pastoral theology.
I. Title.

BV4400.M29   2009
253—dc22
                                                    2008021308

To all refugees, especially the ongoing members of the
Romero House Community,

and the interns and staff who serve these new neighbors through
the leadership of Mary Jo Leddy.

In memory of Margaret Anne Lavin and John McAlpin,
who gifted me with faith, from birth

and Germaine "Mercedes" Donohue, RSM,
who inspired me in ministry, even in death.

CONTENTS

❖

FOREWORD

❖

Christian ministry is often good for those who are served, but is it good for the one who serves? Ministry in the church often transforms others, but can it also transform the life of the minister? Must we be spiritually transformed before we can serve others, or does the experience of service itself transform our hearts and minds? These are the kinds of questions that set the following book in motion. They are questions shared by many today—those who are involved in full-time ministry in the church and those whose Christian service is their daily life and work.

Kathleen McAlpin takes up these questions and unfolds them with great wisdom and experience. Considered one of the most significant resource persons in the church in North America (the United States and Canada), McAlpin has developed a method of contemplative reflection in action that deepens the process of conversion and transformation for those engaged in ministry. This method is situated on sound theological foundations and on the rock of solid and extensive experience in ministry.

McAlpin does not present a blueprint for ministry. Rather, she describes the dynamic of ministry in which simple care for another can lead to one transformation and to another and to another. Ministry lived full-heartedly and reflectively can, she says, lead to a profound spiritual transformation of the one who ministers. Because it is spiritual it also includes a transformation of personal, social, and political perspectives. For McAlpin contemplation is not different from action; it is more than action and is able to lead to deeper action. Contemplation, as she describes it, leads us into reality instead of away from it.

This book draws together McAlpin's many years of experience as a spiritual director and as the director of programs of spirituality and ministry. It specifically draws on her experience with the team members of a small social justice project called Romero House. She taught us a method of contemplative reflection on our experience and moved us all to a deeper level of discipleship. Some of our reflections may not apply to any and every context, but much of the wisdom within this method will.

Mary Jo Leddy, Spring 2007
Regis College and Romero House, Toronto

ACKNOWLEDGMENTS

❖

This book is the fruit of years of study, reflection, and ministry with many gifted people. I cannot name them individually, but I wish to mention a few who collectively supported and encouraged me. I begin with great gratitude for the Institute of the Sisters of Mercy of the Americas, particularly for the leadership and friendships of the former Merion Region of the Mid-Atlantic Community of Mercy. The loving support of my family and friends sustained our relationship over time and distance. This book is steeped in their affection, for which I am extremely grateful. I am also deeply appreciative of the community of Regis College of the Toronto School of Theology for the genuine interest of staff, students, teaching assistants, and faculty. The trust and growth of the Integration for Ministry Seminar participants confirmed the transformative possibilities of this Contemplative Theological Reflection. I am profoundly indebted to the interns and staff of Romero House for their contemplation on life and service with and for the Romero House community of refugees.

Mary Jo Leddy, director of Romero House, has been a collaborator and editor-friend par excellence for this project. The generous invitation from Margaret Brennan, to write in her "monastery," provided a contemplative space to work as well as constant encouragement from her and her local community. The exceptional teaching on theological reflection by Evelyn and James Whitehead and Mary Ellen Sheehan has had a major influence on this work. Heather Gamester's fine editorial contribution was very significant. Nick

Nolan, who witnessed and assessed the Romero House reflection process, was a source of deep inspiration. Joseph Hartzler, Angela McAuliffe, and Kathryn Perry were important and helpful readers. Finally, I am very grateful for the excellent work and dedicated staff of Liturgical Press.

INTRODUCTION

❖

The story of the conversion of Paul on the road to Damascus is paradigmatic in the Christian consciousness. It suggests a sudden, total, and definitive conversion to a different way of life. There are some, perhaps only a few, who experience this kind of dramatic, once-and-forever conversion.

However, there are other stories in the gospels, such as the stories that follow upon the call of the first women and men disciples, that suggest a process of conversion that is more ongoing and multilayered. Dorothy Day, Thomas Merton, and Etty Hillesum are also examples of this process. For every experience of transfiguration there are others of doubt and denial. The meaning of the call of Jesus was not always clear to the disciples. Indeed, it was only after Jesus had left them that they began to understand the meaning of their call to ministry.

It is unfortunate that we often interpret the stories of the first disciples in ways that suggest that we must first experience a definitive conversion to Christ before we can engage in ministry to others. This can lead us to hesitate, often for a long time, before we accept the call to become involved in Christian service. Is anyone ever that transformed by an encounter with Jesus?

This book offers an alternative approach. It suggests that it is through the process of ministering itself that we are converted in an ongoing way. It is not necessary to be transformed before we become contemplative or do justice. It is in the service of others that we become contemplative and, even, Christian.

1

There is nothing automatic about this, and a great deal depends on how we reflect on the experience of the ministry in which we are engaged. We may undergo the experience, as T. S. Eliot suggests, but miss the meaning of it![1] The process of theological reflection is like exploring what lies beneath the surface of an iceberg; there is so much more than what appears on the surface. You could say that theological reflection has the potential to become the contemplative dimension of action.

Over many years I have ministered in education in many Catholic settings—in schools, in parishes, in the formation of people joining religious communities, in spiritual direction ministry, and, more recently, in facilitating the Integration for Ministry theological reflection process at Regis College in Toronto. In this latter setting, I have had the privilege of working with people who are actively engaged in experiences of life and ministry from many religious traditions. I have witnessed how they have been profoundly transformed by their engagements—whether it be in retreat houses, on the streets, in hospitals, in their homes, at food banks, in boardrooms, in personal and societal relationships.

I also know that this transformation is deepened and integrated as they begin to reflect more consciously about the process in which they are engaged. The process of theological reflection is an integral part of their ongoing conversion in the context of Christian life, service, and ministry.

To better indicate how theological reflection is such an important part of the conversion process, I have divided this book into two parts.

In part 1 I will describe a process of theological reflection I have used with a number of groups, especially matured adult students who are integrating their experience of life, ministry, and theological studies. In doing so, I have tried to be attentive to the practice of contemplation and to the more recent developments in the area of adult learning, particularly the processes intended for continuous and transformative learning.

I have chosen as a practical and comprehensible model of contemplative theological reflection my work with a group of people who were engaged in living with and working for refugees in the Romero House community.

Romero House is a community that provides housing and other services for refugees living in four multiple-dwelling buildings in the west end of Toronto. This spirited community is named after the martyred Archbishop Oscar Romero of El Salvador, and practices his vision of *acompanamiento*: "stand by the people." Romero House plays a critical role as an extended family for people at a very vulnerable time in their lives. Through the commitment of the staff, interns, and volunteers, Romero House has provided housing, settlement, and advocacy services for over 4,500 individuals and families since its inception in 1992.[2]

I believe the reflection of this community does stand the test of time as a design for integration and transformation.

In part 2 you will read of the transformation that took place between and among some members of the Romero House community over the course of a six-month reflection process, and be inspired by their courage and generosity. You will meet very real people—Elizabeth who pondered the indignities that could be experienced by using a food bank, and Shawn who questioned the values of the government in light of the gospel—to name two. Some of you will recognize your own questions, issues, and hopes articulated through these people. Whether or not this is so, you will be able to identify with their faith, which sought to understand the summoning of the Spirit in the midst of their committed service. You may choose to read chapter 3 first to meet this community committed to love of neighbor.

In this part, I describe the four component parts of this model of theological reflection: Contemplating Experience, Exploring the Context, Reflecting from and with the Faith Tradition, and Integrating Spirituality into the Reflection Process. The response to this process is the decision for Ongoing Conversion. Here it will be obvious that I have taken some elements from the insights of James and Evelyn Whitehead and Mary Ellen Sheehan and developed them into a transformative process, a process I offer as a contemplative model.

Following these reflections, I will offer some further reflections on the importance of theological reflection in the ministerial process itself. How this reflection is done is every bit as important as what one is doing in ministry. My experience with the Romero House volunteers (and other groups) has helped me understand that attentiveness to how the Spirit works within oneself and others will determine whether ministry is just a job one can master or a summons to the process of growth in the life of a Christian.

Fidelity to this process of theological reflection can move us beyond some of the dichotomies people sometimes experience in ministry. For example, we can see doing the works of mercy or engaging in the struggle for justice as two very different Christian options. The Romero House experience shows that it was the practice of mercy, and the subsequent reflection on this, which led the members to struggle for justice. The persons I have worked with in writing this book concerning ongoing conversion have increased my faith and hope in the living presence of God in the context of a world in crisis and in need of compassion.

It is my deep belief that this process of contemplative theological reflection on the human experiences encountered in ministry can release the "spiritual energy" essential in today's pluralistic and multi-faith society. This is an age of ever-changing pastoral and theological concerns, many of which are overwhelming in magnitude. As many Christians struggle today for identity and meaning, this theological reflection process can help them discover meaning in a culture gripped by meaninglessness.

This book concludes with an extensive bibliography and two appendices. Appendix 1 offers samples of topics and questions for the contemplative theological reflection journal in which participants in the process record their reflections. Appendix 2 sets out the Contemplative Reflection Model and flow chart I have developed through the processes listed in parts 1 and 2.

PART 1

THEOLOGICAL AND EDUCATIONAL ASSUMPTIONS

Chapter 1

INTRODUCTION TO THEOLOGICAL REFLECTION

❖

Let me begin with these questions: What is theological reflection? What is ministry? This chapter introduces theological reflection as a way of doing theology and suggests the value of a contemplative perspective for this process.

What Is Theological Reflection?

Theological reflection is a way of doing theology that starts from the experiences of life and leads to searching in faith, for deeper meaning, and for the living God. However, it is deciding how to live out of this reflective search that is the critical intention of the process of theological reflection.

Theological reflection places the reflector in conversation with other sources of the revelation of God, primarily the faith tradition of the person or community. The world context of the experience is also particularly revelatory of meaning and the living God. The faith tradition and spirituality of the reflector are additional significant sources revealing the experience of God. Critical conversation among the sources is a process by which clarification, differences, or insights mutually challenge and expand each other. From this deepened awareness of God's presence in the experience, decisions are made for more relevant and prophetic choices in ministry. Through this critical conversation the reflector is often challenged to a response of conversion of heart, mind, and action.

What Is Ministry?

Thomas O'Meara defines Christian ministry as the "public activity of a baptized follower of Jesus Christ flowing from the Spirit's charism and an individual personality on behalf of a Christian community to witness to, serve and realize the kingdom of God."[1]

I believe that the groups I work with participate in this transformative definition of ministry. The word ministry may not be a meaningful term for everyone; however, many women and men in Christian service believe themselves to be "disciples of Jesus," responding in "compassionate service," while trying to "do justice" in society. Some may call this ministry while others name it as discipleship or service.

The Romero House community preferred the term *discipleship* to *ministry*. They did not envision themselves as part of the ministry of the institutional church. Along with many today, they question the professionalization of service. When I speak of their experience throughout this book, I will honor their request. However, when I speak generally of the topic of service, I will use the term ministry, as it is applicable to a wide range of services in the tradition of the Christian faith.

It might be good at this point to explore the meaning of the term "ministry" as it is used in the Christian tradition today. A Christian theology of ministry looks to the person of Jesus Christ and how he lived his life as a response to God and God's dream for all of creation. He often referred to this as the reign of God.

Spirituality is a way of living life from what is believed in faith. A "spirituality of Christian ministry" is a living response to God and this dream. In living out this spirituality, I believe that those engaged in compassionate ministry are summoned into a process of ongoing conversion. Through this transformation they participate in extending the reign of God, the vision of Jesus for the world. In this context, I see a spirituality of ministry as a way in which a community of Christians engages in compassionate service.

THEOLOGICAL REFLECTION AND THEOLOGY OF MINISTRY

Since the time of Anselm in the eleventh century, theology has been defined as faith seeking understanding. Currently, theological reflection may be described as an effort to respond to the search for the living God and the faith questions arising out of the context of the world in which we live. A response to this process is a summons to transformation.

Theology will continue to change as the context of history and the consciousness of our experiences develop. In Albert Nolan's words, "theology has become a way of nourishing faith and strengthening hope by reflecting upon the presence of God in our context."[2] Life changes and so does reflection on life.

> Our ever-changing minds engage with the ever-changing faith experience of the Church community within the ever-changing context of human history and we create ever-changing patterns of theological understanding like kaleidoscope configurations which are coherent in themselves and ever beautiful but which are never stationary or final.[3]

The pattern of doing ministry is one example of our changing context in the task of doing a theology of ministry.

For a theological reflection on ministry to be credible, I found it important to be both critical and contemplative. Mary Ellen Sheehan contributes to a method of critical theological reflection on ministry in which she suggests a careful correlation of the reflecting person's

- lived experience,
- cultural context,
- faith tradition, and
- operative spirituality.

These sources of critical reflection are essential to the theological reflection process I developed and refined with the Romero House community. I also found the contemplative stance in Thomas O'Meara's method of reflecting on a theology of ministry to be quite compelling. It was important for me to integrate a contemplative perspective with a critical design for theological reflection.

THEOLOGY OF MINISTRY
FROM A CONTEMPLATIVE PERSPECTIVE

O'Meara sees theology of ministry as a meditation in which we become aware of a "revelation from God about ourselves." This revelation has the power to move us toward the memory of Jesus of Nazareth and toward the contemporary world of others. During meditation we gain self-knowledge, remember the life of Jesus, and are connected to the lives of others.[4] Meditation also leads us to contemplation of God's Spirit living on in human history. This approach moves the development of theology from a theoretical study about God to a process of prayerful meditation seeking the presence of God in life and discerning a response to this revelation. Valuing meditation, as a way of doing a theology of ministry, convinced me to include prayerful contemplation as an integral component of theological reflection.

Brian McDermott explains the term *contemplative* in this regard:

> By "contemplative" I am not referring to a deep mystical experience, but rather the kind of relationship with God in which you are able to notice what God is like and what God is doing, be affected by it, notice how one is affected, and respond to God out of that awareness.[5]

This description allowed our group to perceive a compassionate God affecting each member of the group and calling forth a committed response to this revelation.

John Haughey contributes to an understanding of this integration by valuing the role of prayer and conversion in a theological reflection process.[6] Haughey believes that the dynamics of human knowing (attending, understanding, judging, and deciding) enable a person or a group to move from inauthenticity to authenticity, which he notes is Bernard Lonergan's definition of conversion. He believes that prayer, as a human activity, can function as a religious contribution to theological reflection by consciously seeking the presence of God.

Theological reflection builds on Lonergan's dynamics of human knowing. These dynamics include attending to the data of the situation, understanding and interpreting the theology of the situation, judging and analyzing the deeper issues and the cultural context, and deciding the meaning and the response required of the situation. For an integrated experience of knowing, these four dynamics embody the affective level as well as the intellectual level and lead to a decision.[7] This dynamic sets a path for ongoing conversion.

CONCLUSION

Doing theological reflection with the Romero community increased each participant's faith and hope in the living presence of God and called forth conversion in the context of life. A passion for faith and a contemplative openness to the presence of God and to self-knowledge were valuable transformative resources.

Chapter 2

THEOLOGICAL REFLECTION AS A TRANSFORMATIVE PROCESS

❖

INTRODUCTION

Theological reflection is a transformative path for ongoing conversion. To substantiate this I will review relevant theories of transformative learning and correlate these with theological reflection, for the one, in concert with the other, can assist in the process of ongoing conversion in the Christian community.

Simply stated, theological reflection is a process used by Christians to become aware of the living God in the context of daily life. Through this process, communities of faith and individuals reflect on their experiences and notice the presence of God at work in their lives and in society. From this awareness, although they see the brokenness of the world, they also see the hope of God for humankind. These beliefs and spiritual resources give them the wisdom to look closely and critically at their world, and help them to discern a response to given situations, and thus participate in the reign of God.

I was introduced to theological reflection in the mid-1970s through the early mentoring of James and Evelyn Whitehead as they taught their "method in ministry." Briefly described, their model represents the interaction among three poles of a triangle and is thus named the Tri-polar Model of Theological Reflection. Each pole represents a source of information for reflection: (1) experience, (2) tradition, and (3) culture.[1]

This dynamic triangle offers a method by which to develop skills in attending, asserting, and decision making. In this model of theological reflection, *attending* is a way of paying careful attention to the religious dimension in a given reality in ministry. This awareness enables one to discern and decide the ongoing relationship between faith and action. *Assertion* is the skill by which a mature Christian engages the Word of God with other sources of information. A renewed faith perspective from this encounter is at the heart of ministerial decision making and reveals the potential for ongoing conversion. In theological reflection, *decision making* is the moment when one's discernment leads to changed attitudes or concrete actions. The triple dialogue of experience, culture, and tradition witnesses to the presence of God in the event considered and influences decision making in the process. I now call this decision making for change the process of ongoing conversion in the life of a minister or community of faith. I have used this model of theological reflection in a variety of ministry experiences for almost twenty years.

In the early 1990s Mary Ellen Sheehan presented me with a perspective on theological reflection that enabled me to develop an operative theology while uncovering God's healing presence in the human experience. Sheehan describes theological reflection as a method that integrates theological knowledge, pastoral experience, and faith commitment.[2] She adds spirituality to her sources of reflection and uses the term "context" instead of the Whiteheads' term, "culture."

THEOLOGY OF MINISTRY: A PASSIONATE WORK OF FAITH

Sheehan summarizes her method by suggesting that theology is a "passionate work" of faith engaged in a project, a process, and a product. Her own words best describe her belief about this dynamic understanding of doing theology:

- the project of theology is to know, love, and beat with the heart of God who is intimately related in love with the human community;

- the process of theology is the sustained and never-ending mutual, critical correlation of context, tradition, and spirituality in order to expose the biases and blockages that exist in each of these poles, and also to identify the truths and values that are alive in them, to garner energy for new theory and transformational action;
- the product of theology is a more adequate theory and practice through which our way of being in the world as human community will be more like God's way of being. In the words of Jesus, this is to live in the *basileia* or kinship family of God.[3]

This dynamic understanding of theology is fittingly applied to the process of doing a theology of ministry.

Sheehan's description of the project of theology articulates a clear motivation for engaging in ministry. To live and love with the heart of God is a deep desire I share with many people of faith engaged in ministry.

Moving to the process of theology, Sheehan describes theological reflection as a process of correlation, or reflective conversation, with reflection on four critical sources. To repeat, the sources for reflection are: human experience, context of experience, espoused faith tradition, and operative spirituality. Reflection upon and critical correlation of these sources enables both bias and truth to be revealed and opens one to ongoing transformation. Critical correlation is a way of reflecting on experience with an active conversation among sources of crucial information. From this reflection, truth can unlock prejudices and enable a change in attitude, in practice, or in response to life.

The product of theology is the fruit of reflection and critical correlation that leads to transformation of theory and practice. This is known as praxis in ministry. I believe the product of theological reflection contributes to the gift of ongoing conversion in the life and service of compassionate ministers.

This passionate work of doing theology of ministry invites a reflection on the initial words of Jesus' ministry, which were a call to repentance and conversion (Mark 1:15; Matt 4:17). Christian conversion is a turn from one way of living to living the reign of

God (*basileia tou Theou*). *Basileia* was central to Jesus' understanding of mission, as God's desire for all to live as the family of God. This desire became central to Jesus' life of ministry.[4]

This process was basic to the method I used for theological reflection with the Romero House community. However, I found the contemplative stance in Thomas O'Meara's method of doing a theology of ministry and the prophetic dimension in the work of David Tracy to be quite compelling. It was important for me to integrate their contributions into my own process of theological reflection.

FURTHER SOURCES FOR THEOLOGICAL REFLECTION

The theological work of the Whiteheads and Sheehan were at the root of the theological reflection process I prepared for the Romero House group. Although the participants did not consider themselves skilled in theology, they were able to articulate well their questions, understandings, and spirituality, as they reflected on the commitment they have to working with refugees. To aid them in the theological reflection process, I encouraged them to reflect on their experience with the refugees, the context of this experience, their faith tradition, and their practice of spirituality. In addition to assisting the participants to narrate their experiences of life with the refugees, it was helpful to suggest to them some examples of context, tradition, and spirituality as sources for reflection:

- *Context* is the relationship between the experience one brings to reflection and the world surrounding that experience. Contextual realities include such variables as the socioeconomic location, background, the historical-political reality, the sacredness of creation, geographic space and time, interpersonal dynamics, cultural values and symbols, myths, folklore, literature, art, and movements, and trends such as multiculturalism, postmodernism, and feminism. It is critical in a social analysis of the reality to question who benefits and who is burdened in a particular context.

- *Tradition* is the relationship between the reflection on experience and Sacred Scripture, truths, wisdom, and the theological teachings of the faith. It would also include the religious heritage and other theological themes such as creation, grace, sin, redemption, or meaningfulness.

• *Spirituality* is the relationship between the way we live and the faith we have internalized from our tradition. It is the human desire to integrate all life with a lived experience of God. For Christians, the experience of God is in the presence of the Holy Spirit revealed in Jesus, the Christ. An expression of Christian spirituality is the desire to live a life reflecting the values of gospel discipleship.

In theological reflection, questions are brought to the experience, the context, the tradition, and the spirituality of the reflector:

1. Because of the value of seeking the living God we ask: "How does each source reveal the presence of God?"
2. Because of our human condition we ask: "How do we respond to or resist God's presence?" "Who benefits and who is burdened in this context?"
3. Because of the possibility of ongoing conversion we ask: "What is the invitation or summons of Spirit in this situation?"

Interpreting the related dimensions of human experience and the sources of information is central to theological reflection. The Whiteheads are clear that leaving out any one of the dimensions can lead to a breakdown in the reflection process. Omitting the cultural context can yield a *fundamentalist* interpretation of the reflection. If the faith tradition and spirituality are not included in the dialogue, a *secular* interpretation of the situation may result. If personal experience is not a component of the correlation process, a purely *theoretical* interpretation of the process may arise.[5]

Theological reflection ensures that the fruit of ongoing conversion is not flawed by fundamental, secular, or theoretical interpretations.

THEORIES OF TRANSFORMATIVE LEARNING

Three theories of transformation situate theological reflection as a sound educational method leading to conversion: (1) transformative learning, (2) the reflective practitioner, and (3) the contemplative practitioner.

The effectiveness of these theories is reflected in the experiences of the Romero House participants who were surprised and shocked when they observed the harsh treatment the refugees received when they accompanied them or pleaded on their behalf to an agency that was expected to be one of service. Much reflection followed such encounters, experienced members helping to confirm the intuitions of the newer volunteers. Wisdom was gained from critical reflection and dialogue. The theological reflection process assisted them in dealing with understanding the ambiguity encountered in each unique situation.

Jack Mezirow defines adult education as a "process of assisting adults to understand the meaning of their experience by participating more fully and freely in reflective and critical discourse to validate expressed ideas."[6] Theological reflection is one such resource for participants, as it helps them to interpret their experience. Their reflections become the material for the research method used to gain wisdom through their reflections.

Transformative Learning

Adults and expectations. Transformative learning is based on the belief that adults learn when they are free to change their expectations and gain new perspectives on life. For adults to grow they need to interpret their personal experiences and life situations in new ways and to become free to engage in a process of transformation. Expectations gained from past experiences govern how adults comprehend new realities. Adults develop habits around expectations that strongly influence their perceptions. From these expectations they maintain certain perspectives that give meaning to their reality. It is necessary to be aware of these expectations and to be able to appreciate and to comprehend new experiences from fresh perspectives to learn.

Mezirow describes "making meaning" as a dynamic of learning. He notes that adults initially learn through socialization, an unconscious way of understanding the world. From this early experience, culturally determined and unconscious perspectives are carried into the adult world. These perspectives are often inadequate, and adults are challenged, through the complexity of life, to look at new experiences from a different perspective to gain new meaning.

New learning evolves where unreflected interpretations no longer work. Critically examining our interpretations, particularly emotional reactions of shock or surprise, and the perspectives they express is the major imperative of modern adulthood.[7] The awareness of and the capacity to change perspectives are foundational to the process of ongoing Christian conversion.

Transformative learning imagines new insights and appropriates new interpretations. Through a process of reflection and discourse, new insights and interpretations guide adults into new awareness, new feelings, and alternative actions.

The value of reflection. Fostering reflective and transformative learning should be the cardinal goal of adult education.[8] Reflection involves examining the assumptions arising from each experience, through careful consideration of the reliability of these assumptions, our beliefs, and our emotional reactions.

Learning the skill of reflection helps adults reinterpret biases and assists in decisions about mindful living of values and beliefs. Reflection helps overcome the power of distortion and gives new meaning to life. It transforms interpretations and empowers adults to understand the self and one's perspective and to engage in transformative learning. To my mind it is the core of this process.

Transformation of consciousness. Through transformative learning, adults are freed from influences that limit options and rational control over life. Learning to be free of distorted thoughts and feelings is consistent with the freedom needed in the process of ongoing conversion. Transformative learning leads to a transformation of consciousness.

Theological reflection evokes transformation and moves toward an active response to insights gained from reflection. Although the process of theological reflection is a substantial method of transformative learning, insights learned through self-reflection can be distorted. That is why dialogue with those we know best can help validate our assertions and ways of acting and change how we interpret feelings. Dialogue supports the conversational component of the theological reflection process and helps to avoid distorted thinking.

Individual and societal transformation. Working together, members of a group are capable of transforming the perspective of the group and in turn influence social, cultural, and societal life. Group thinking that is unquestioning and loyalty that is uncritical will hinder societal transformation. Questioning minds and constructive criticism can assure cultural reformation and influence change for a better society.

This transformation was evident within the Romero group. I observed a depth of change in individuals and the transformation of the group as a whole that has continued to the cultural reformation of the refugee community in Toronto. Critical reflection and discourse created an atmosphere for possible transformation for both the individual and the group.

The Reflective Practitioner

The art of learning through reflection-in-action. Donald Schon believes that curricula covering areas from computers to health care have not prepared students to deal with the conflicts, the complexities, and the justice issues they will encounter in their practices. As an alternative to additional technical knowledge and rational instruction, Schon suggests that adults learn from the wisdom and "artistry" of competent practitioners through internship programs. These programs offer vital learning tools for everyone from medical practitioners to counselors, plumbers, biologists, computer programmers, and ministers. Here students examine how competent practitioners handle uncertainty, uniqueness, challenging situations, and conflicts in value. Schon is interested in how extraordinary practitioners acquire their competency and how adults can best learn from them.[9]

From the reflections and dialogue of the newer Romero House volunteers, it is evident that they learn through their interaction with the more experienced staff. The theological reflection process provides a deeper reflection and dialogue to add to the artistry of learning what it means to engage in the ministry of refugee resettlement in Canada.

Reflection moves to artistry. Reflection on critical questions gives rise to new ideas and creative possibilities that continue the cycle of surprise, reflection, and experimentation. "This kind of reflection-in-action is central to the artistry with which practitioners sometimes make new sense of uncertain, unique or conflicted situations."[10] Reflection-in-action enables the learner to respond creatively and to trust to intuitive moments when theory and practice come together.

I observed that the artistry of hope was a strong lesson mutually learned by the participants, for as bureaucrats failed to respond to urgent needs of the refugees, in the midst of conflicted situations, the participants intuitively clarified values and created resources from the neighbors and supporters of Romero House. They received hope from a network of committed persons known to be concerned about the world of refugees. They learned that for a neighborhood to welcome a refugee it takes understanding, creativity, and hope for the future. They learned from the refugees themselves, who maintained hope despite the political turmoil of their countries of origin and the difficulties inherent in their daily transition into a new life.

The Contemplative Practitioner

A movement from reflection to contemplation. The definition John Miller gives to adult education is the "release of the human heart."[11] He believes that this release is fostered by the contemplative practice of meditation. As an educator, Miller brings the value of contemplation to teachers in their roles as practitioners. I was amazed to find that he engages students in the practice of contemplation during class in a public university.

Miller believes that a good adult educator has developed a way of knowing through contemplation that reveals a depth of character he calls *Being* or *Presence*. This contemplative practice of meditating on experience and Scripture was an important component of the theological reflection process in which we engaged at Romero House. It is remarkable to note that liberation, union, and compassion were elements in the participants' reflections, for Miller teaches that these qualities are the fruit of meditation.

Contemplation, according to Miller, is a non-dualistic state of consciousness that involves a union of all that is fundamental to life. Through contemplation, the adult becomes one with reality; the world of goodness and truth is available to the heart. In this process of openness, Miller notes, one develops compassionate attention and wholeness within the self and with the earth.

It is clear to Miller that awareness through meditation is a stance that can infuse all of one's being and doing. One begins to live with a sense of an "awakened heart." He believes that this basic stance of compassionate attention and connectedness can be part of everyday living. In tune with this theory, I consciously included periods of meditation in the "reflection-on-ministry" for the Romero House participants, who were always grateful for the time to stop, to reflect, and to be mindful of their experiences and the faith that gives them hope in the midst of their struggles for compassion and justice.

This theory is a witness to me for my practice of ministry and a further inducement to use a contemplative approach in the process of theological reflection. It was evident that the participants received both inspiration and courage from their contemplation on the mysteries of the Scriptures and *the* Christian myth, the parable of Jesus. Their contemplative reflections moved them toward compassion, not only for the refugees, but also for themselves.

THE CORRELATION BETWEEN TRANSFORMATIVE LEARNING AND THEOLOGICAL REFLECTION

Since transformation through a search for meaning is considered the most important task for adult learners, transformation in the meaning of faith is important for those in formation for adult ministry. The task here, then, is the reflection on ongoing conversion through a search for meaning in the context of service.

Mezirow's theory of transformation helps me to understand how the process of change is based on transformation of expectations and perspectives. When adults reflect on their experiences and assumptions, the process enables them to develop new perspectives on reality. By casting off old assumptions, they are free to change, a central aspect of conversion. This is the essence of this study.

Meaning evolves through an acceptance of the self and brings a new awareness of the current reality. For instance, the evolution of changed perspectives and new meaning was evident at Romero House as the members of the group participated in the reflection process. It was obvious that some participants moved from an awareness of deep anger or sadness to a new sense of compassion. For others, there was also an evolution from discouragement to hope as new perspectives evolved. However, some developments were not as positive. Some experienced a loss of confidence in certain social services, and the meaningfulness of government support diminished for most of the participants. It appeared that some of their initial assumptions, or trust in the political system, were misguided. As the process moved on to the communal experience, they seemed to balance this loss of meaning with a more realistic and responsible sense of self-reliance and collaborative involvement.

Perspective transformation and new awareness leads one toward integration. Self-integration is a process that enables actions or decisions to come from a reinterpretation of experiences. As Mezirow contends, true transformation of consciousness carries over into responsible action. Decision making is incorporated into the process of theological reflection.

Groups involved in transformative education and action for a better society reflect the emergence of a power that was certainly evident in this reflection group. Critical discourse is integral to transformation and the presence of honesty in group conversation. New meaning gained from individual and communal reflection leads to transformative learning. I saw this group gain new energy as it engaged in dialogue, appropriated new perspectives, and continued to commit itself to societal conversion.

Reflection-in-action and theological reflection. Schon's contribution to adult education is his critique of the professional model.[12] Along with technical, rational training, a learner is placed with an "artist" who "reflects on a practice" and mentors the learner. Moment-to-moment insight during a given experience is passed along. Reflection following a skillful task is shared with the learner.[13] Learning from guided practice is an operative dynamic of the Romero House community.

I believe that the theological reflection process carried these participants from action-in-ministry to reflection-in-ministry. The group passed on wisdom from their shared experiences of relationships with the refugees, of service to them, and of their frustrations with the political system. Since much of the work during the theological reflection was of an interior nature, there was little expectation that all reflection would be shared. However, as the group grew in confidence, insights from a faith perspective were brought into the conversation.

I found that Schon's call for reflection in practice was important as a foundation for theological reflection on ministry. The reflection group included a mixture of experienced and new members. In their experience with refugees, I witnessed mutual learning in the artistry of service, the expression of compassion, and the works of justice. The group was intergenerational, and this served as a resource for newer members to learn the art of competent and compassionate service in the refugee community. The energy and idealism of the younger members also had a strong influence on the ongoing process of transformation of the group.

The practice of contemplation and theological reflection. As noted above, Miller's contemplative practice of meditating on experience, myths, and mysteries of the tradition, and the inner and outer contexts of events was integral to the theological reflection process of this group. He highlighted the values of "liberation," "union," and "compassion" as the fruits of contemplation, the very values experienced by the participants during the theological reflection process.

In designing this process, it was obvious that establishing connections between theological reflection and the three theories of transformative education was vital to creating a design that could be reflective, transformative, and contemplative.

A DESIGN FOR THEOLOGICAL REFLECTION: EXPERIENCE AND RELIGIOUS EDUCATION—THE FOUR STEPS TOWARD A CONTEMPLATIVE THEOLOGICAL REFLECTION

To explore the inner experiences of the community, I designed a prayerful and contemplative theological reflection process for the Romero House group. Since transformation through a search for meaning is considered the most important task for adult learners, similar transformation is important in exploring adult faith and ministry. In this process I looked at the experience of ongoing conversion, inner and outer, in individuals and in reflecting communities of ministry. I am reminded here of Lonergan's call to reflection on conversion as a possible contribution to the renewal of theology, and in this instance to a renewal of theology of ministry.

The process of theological reflection is the story of ongoing conversion through a search for meaning in the experience of service.

1. The first step of the process is to evoke the thoughts and feelings from a historical incident in the participant's life, in this case experiences of service with the poor and the refugees. The reflecting person is asked to meditate on his or her experience, earnestly consider his or her assumptions, and set aside any prejudgments about his or her experience of the incident. Openness is a classical spiritual discipline and a necessary part of letting go of assumptions.

2. The second step in theological reflection is analysis of the cultural context of the experience. This involves rational and intuitive questions concerning such matters as historical aspects, cultural realities, or the socioeconomic values of the one who is burdened by and the one who benefits from the experience. Themes and symbols are often evident at this

phase in the process. This reflection results in assumptions being confirmed, disconfirmed, or transformed in light of new insights. Fostering an awareness of the context of experiences enables one to become familiar with one's response and one's analysis of the refugee world.

3. The third step is to reflect theologically, with insights of faith from the reinterpreted assumptions. This has the potential to lead one to see deeper meaning in the experience. Theological traditions, issues, and the reality of the experience evoke the capacity to know the sacred in a lived experience. In this process, the participants' reflections varied from a passion for stories of mercy and justice in the lives of prophets to a new enthusiasm for the Gospel call to love of neighbor.

4. The fourth step calls one to reflect on the spirituality of an experience and a conscious decision for transformed action. Spirituality, the lived expression of faith, is relational if one believes in a personal God. The new action may range from a decision to reflect more on the experience, to a response of compassion for the suffering of another, to a change in attitude. The entire person's physical, spiritual, rational, intuitive, and relational capabilities are involved in a decision to respond from a contemplative stance. The responses of the participants included movement from personal anger and political resentment to a decision to accept reality and to work from their commitment to love of neighbor, and practical and prophetic actions rising from compassionate care. Experiences of God varied from distant to empowering.

Using the above steps as the design, the practice of prayer and contemplation throughout the theological reflection process is vital. In this model it was important that the participants spend time meditating on their personal experiences, assumptions, faith, and analysis, to help them to gain wisdom for impending decisions.

Discernment, as a spiritual practice, is prayerful reflection on decision making that flows from the insight gained through meditation and contemplation. It has the potential for movement into fruitful action. This practice is constitutive of the decision-making aspects of theological reflection.

The theological reflection process at Romero House was interrelational, yet each individual was responsible for his or her own inner experience of transformation. The group benefited from aspects of the dialogue and appropriate moments of sharing. There was a quality of respect for the whole experience of each participant. The communal decision flowed from a creative dialogue. A communal gift of grace was apparent in the group. The decision to have a prayer vigil was a political and contemplative gesture in response to the financial cutbacks imposed by the government. The participants were aware of the courage needed to live through a communal suffering with its impending stress and crucifixion of the vulnerable.

The final moment of the theological reflection process was to ritualize and affirm the decision and fruit of the reflection. The participants conscientiously offered their closing symbols. One meaningful symbol was the Amnesty International icon, a candle surrounded by barbed wire. The candle reflects hope and the wire acknowledges sustained suffering. The reflection process ended with a prayer, with each participant holding a candle, lit from one source, representing the Light of the World.

The communal decision was ritualized in the twenty-four-hour vigil at Queen's Park in the downtown core of Toronto.

Did this transformation process of the individuals and of the community of Romero House affect the city of Toronto? We dare to hope so, for the mosaic nature of Canada and the compassionate hospitality the city gives to the world's refugees are in need of continuous transformation. The Romero community contributes to this conversion in its collaboration with the Sanctuary Group and other refugee advocacy groups, and as it continues to relate honestly with the immigration system.

Since my experience at Romero House, I have carried on with a comprehensive study of the above theories. I am convinced of the place of transformation, reflection, and contemplation in adult education and formation for ministry and have created a Contemplative Theological Reflection Process that is transformative in structure.

CONCLUSION

This chapter situates theological reflection within the sound theories of theology and adult education. Theological reflection is a way of approaching theology that integrates the praxis of ministry with theological theory. Adult educational theories that are transformative and contemplative assisted in integrating this practice in ministry with educational theories. An application of this contemplative theological reflection model is described in the following section.

PART 2

APPLICATION OF DESIGN FOR A CONTEMPLATIVE THEOLOGICAL REFLECTION MODEL

Chapter 3

CONTEMPLATING EXPERIENCE

❖

Contemplating experience is the first step in the process of theological reflection and is used to evoke the thoughts and feelings from a historical incident in each participant's life, in this case experiences of service with the poor and the refugees. The reflecting person is asked to meditate on this experience, earnestly consider their assumptions, and set aside any prejudgments about the incident. Openness is a classical spiritual discipline and a necessary part of letting go of assumptions.

INTRODUCTION

In a book entitled *Lonergan and Spirituality: Towards a Spiritual Integration*, Tad Dunne states that "when we listen to the stories people claim are true or significant, we should listen for the presence or absence of conversion."[1]

This chapter introduces the reader to the Romero House group and discusses how they began to reveal their stories, and what their reflections meant to them. Interestingly, almost immediately it became evident that the participants were involved in a process of change or conversion; I will attempt to describe the process of conversion as it emerged "from below."

This experience of ministry began as circle of persons gathered around a kitchen table. It ended four months later with a twenty-four-hour prayer vigil at the provincial government buildings at

Queen's Park in Toronto. This experience led me to consider the dynamic of circles of people as a primary image of ministry.

There were seven participants in this reflective process and each was connected in service of the refugees of the Romero House community. This group supported the refugees in their many practical and emotional needs as they went through the legal procedures required to become landed immigrants of Canada. The Romero setting provides a temporary home and a secure atmosphere, as all anxiously await the determination of their future.

The focus of this process of theological reflection was not the refugees but the group supporting them. The aim of the participants was to reflect on and integrate their experience of service with their life of faith. The goal was to reflect on the influence of service and the grace of ongoing conversion witnessed through the process. Working with the Romero House community provided the incentive for the contemplative theological reflection model I designed and include in appendix 2.

An Introduction to the Participants

Andrew, a married man in his thirties, identified himself as a political activist. He worked as an editor for a Christian justice coalition. Although he was not directly involved in the community of refugees, he did political analysis and lobbying for such issues as legal aid and the Head Tax on refugees, and used what he learned from his justice work to help the staff and refugees of Romero House. Andrew's involvement with Romero House has been mutually beneficial. He experienced support in the study and reflection group, from the Romero community, and through this process of theological reflection. His questions and insights were valuable contributions to both the content and the process of these gatherings.

Darlene came to Toronto from Canada's east coast. A theology student in her early twenties, she realized that her studies needed to be based in the "real world of human experience." She was introduced to the Romero House community by some of the other young volunteers. She was invited to a community barbecue to celebrate the welcoming of new members and to thank the volunteers that year. The hospitality she experienced and her need to be engaged in a community of service drew her to volunteer at Romero House. She decided to apply to the full-time volunteer program and to set aside her theological studies for a year.

Elizabeth, a young university graduate, volunteered as a full-time staff person at Romero House. At first, she saw this as an "opportunity" and "something she just knew she had to do." As her encounter with the refugees evolved, the "opportunity" became a "commitment." Through her experience, she decided to become more actively involved in human rights issues and to focus on human rights law. Elizabeth, a Catholic Christian, was involved in justice initiatives during her university experience. At times she felt "harshness" in some of this work and in those with whom she was collaborating. This harshness shifted in her during her stay at Romero House, where she experienced the work of justice and the practice of "faith" to be mutually beneficial.

Emile, in his late twenties, was a former teacher from Western Canada, where he was a leader in the formation of small Christian communities. He was a member of a lay community associated with a Catholic religious congregation and a full-time volunteer for the Romero community. Emile used his gift as an educator to teach English as a second language to the refugees, his depth of faith to help in the planning for the liturgical celebrations of the community, and his skills in justice work and community building to work for the welfare of the refugees.[2]

Mary Jo, a founding member of Romero House and now its director, is a committed woman of faith who has been active in the work of justice and peace for many years. She is involved in higher education and has a strong background in philosophy and theology. Through her leadership, the staff and volunteers of Romero House address the housing and immigration needs of the refugees. Mary Jo's vision leads her to encourage all members to be part of a mutual community of neighbors and faith.

Shawn, a young man in his late twenties, converted from New Age spirituality to Christianity during his high school years. He discovered that there was shallowness to the New Age movement, and he was attracted to a depth he perceived in the spirituality of Christianity. He spent his early twenties studying and working hard to get enough money to travel. He accepted uninspiring jobs as a laborer for as long as it took to get what he needed to take off for distant lands. His last European escapade ended in a prolonged stay of about six months on the Isle of Iona off the coast of Scotland. There he lived with a "strong, justice-minded, multicultural Christian community." His Celtic wanderlust was stabilized by the monastic lifestyle of this community. When he returned from this last venture, he wondered how he could integrate a new form of monasticism with a spirituality of justice and service. Life in a small, conservative prairie town was very frustrating for him.

"After a forceful argument with [his parents] over the distribution of wealth," his father asked him what *he* (Shawn) was doing for the poor of Canada. This challenged him to do something about his anger over the injustices he witnessed, instead of just complaining about them. He remembered the stories he had heard during his last year at university about the refugees and the Romero volunteer program. The contemporary icon of Nike running shoes and the sound-bite phrase inspired him to "Just Do It." He left home and joined the Romero House community.

Winki, the senior member of the theological reflection group, is a mature Christian woman who was a nurse administrator of a chronic care hospital that recently closed because of government cutbacks. In her early nursing experience, she was a lay missionary in West Africa. Her recent work was with patients who were severely disabled, both physically and mentally.

A number of years ago, Winki volunteered at Romero House because she needed "to be in touch with well people." At the same time she wanted "to take some action in the lives of vulnerable people in our society." She began by visiting one woman and her children at Romero House and gradually became a trusted friend of all the refugees. She became a committed volunteer, a facilitator of the Romero Women's Group, and a member of the Romero House board of directors.

The Dynamics of Ongoing Conversion

From the participants' responses to the process of theological reflection, it became clear to me that conversion had been under way in each of them before their involvement in Romero House. And it was evident also that this process of conversion had been deepened and extended through their participation in the reflection sessions. There were indicators of changes in perspective, beliefs, emotions, relationships, and commitments, as well as in attitudes toward political-social structures. Critical reflection on their experiences, ideas, and beliefs, and the realities of risk taking, helped the participants to turn from previously held perspectives and positions to challenging new ones.

I would name this development *Christian ongoing conversion*. *Christian* because "it is characterized by a specifically religious quality—a relationship to God in the person of Jesus Christ."[3] *Conversion* because of the "change of heart that results from hearing the good news of salvation (through Jesus Christ) and God's offer of love."[4] *Ongoing* because the participants daily counted on God's offer of love to "face and acknowledge the consequences of their initial option."[5]

Being with this group and working with them on their reflections was continually inspiring. The idealism of those in early stages of commitment was in sharp contrast to those who reflected the fruit of faithful years of labor for the reign of God. Each revealed "threads" of ongoing conversion.

An initial thread of ongoing conversion for this group was very relational. Early on in the reflection experience it was clear that the participants valued relationships with the persons they met in service. Most, upon reflection, experienced God in this setting of service, while one initially struggled with experiencing a relationship with God. Each grew in self-awareness as the reflection process unfolded. Other conversion threads evolved in a movement from doing the works of mercy to compassionate service and developing a deeper desire for justice. The final thread of ongoing conversion was a summons to live the mandate of Christian love.

Participation in this dynamic process of human and spiritual conversion had four dimensions, as listed below:

1. Ongoing Conversion in Relationship to Self, Others, and God
2. Ongoing Conversion in Compassionate Service: The Works of Mercy
3. Ongoing Conversion in the Deeper Desire for Justice
4. Ongoing Conversion to Christian Love

Of course, these dimensions cannot be neatly classified as they are individual and intimate, although they can be identified. Let's look at some threads of conversion taken from the reflections of the participants. Although data is available for every category from each person, I have made selections that are most indicative of conversion. Selected threads vary in strength and texture according to the life experience and personality of each. My point is not to make moral judgments about the conversion in the lives of the particular participants but to present findings that pertain to the relationship between conversion and ministry, to give examples that best illustrate the four dimensions of the process of conversion.

ONGOING CONVERSION IN MINISTRY

As noted earlier, critical correlation of experience with the sources of context, tradition, and spirituality opens one to transformation. The process of theological reflection through which this correlation is made reveals both bias and truth. Truth can enable a change in attitude, practice, or response in life, and participation in the process of ongoing conversion.

As the facilitator of this process, it was obvious to me that I would encounter some biases, while reflecting on the sources of context, theology, and spirituality with the participants.

In reflecting on the political context, for instance, I knew that a balanced budget is a wise fiscal policy. However, I sympathized with the reflection group, who saw no merit in government policies that reduced the budget by discriminating against "the other." The drastic and immediate cutbacks of 21 percent that occurred at the time of this study and affected the poor, the elderly, and the afflicted, most of whom were women and children, were a serious concern.

It is true that care for the disadvantaged is a gospel imperative and not a bias, but at the same time I knew it is unwise to block out the voice of the government while discerning a response to this reality. Because of my stance of political suspicion, my biases, and my passion for the underprivileged, I was liable to be uninformed or misinformed in my judgments. In light of this reflection, it is important that, while ministering as a facilitator, I did not so align myself with the rhetoric of the group that I was unable to help them to discern their reflections.

In the process of reflection on the tradition of the church, I continued to have a favorable bias regarding the model of church as a community of faith and ministry, as a discipleship of equals. This value continued to raise questions around the institutional and patriarchal reality of the church. For me, the value of loving criticism, awareness of the wisdom of the tradition, and the discernment of right relationships are all part of the ongoing conversion of the practice of ministry. As I attended to the group and their reflection, I had to be aware of my biases, and strive to understand the perspective of the group or individuals within the group.

The need for ongoing conversion was also evident from my reflections on spirituality. It is clear that I see many realities of God's love through the lens of compassion or mercy. This limits my perspective and can sway the interpretation of this reflection. Staying close to the direct words and experience of the reflections of the group prevented me from projecting onto their reality or limiting their reflections to the perspective of my spirituality.

Ongoing Conversion in Relationship to Self, Others, and God

Throughout this reflection, as the participants contemplated and reflected on their experiences, their relationships among themselves, with others, and with God evolved into deeper understandings, firmer commitments, and more meaningful significance.

Winki: Important to be with the vulnerable and the poor. When Winki started to visit Romero House, she met Senait, an Eritrean woman and her children. Winki noted that she was moved by this woman "who opened my heart to her generosity." She was touched by Senait's "overwhelming sense of life for her many children." Although out of immediate danger, her family continued to be vulnerable to the Canadian immigration system. Winki's "hope was to be a support to this woman and her children. [She] had no idea of the degree of their vulnerability or how protracted it would be." Yet, as this case unfolded, Winki remained committed to the family with her love and care.

Winki reflected on another story of her relationship with a young Somali "woman who had been a victim of war." Her own words best recount the story:

> A quiet (silent) Somali young woman, who sat and smiled through an hour of chat about nutrition, shopping, etc., that followed a cooking session in the kitchen—shyly talked with another young woman from her country who participated in the afternoon gathering. They both left the room as we were having tea . . . a few minutes later the person who had been chatting came to get me to "see" the young woman who was a new arrival. She was in her room, sitting on her bed, her skirt lifted to show us a badly injured stump of a leg that had been amputated. She was full of shrapnel. The prosthesis was not fitted well and was very painful for her. She continued to smile as her story came out. There was one of us on each side of her as she held us and rocked back and forth telling us a small piece of her story.

Winki "felt totally inadequate" in the face of the pain and situation of this young woman. She hoped that as a community they "could help her physically, and gradually mend some of her deeper wounds together" for she was moved by the strength of these vulnerable women. She demonstrated her ongoing conversion by co-creating a community of care with them. Winki's dedication contributed to the caring and sustaining strength of the Romero Women's Group.

It was their commitment to these relationships that moved Winki to respond as she did when the financial cutbacks were announced. On that day, the woman's group asked the question: "How will we feed our kids?" In the absence of an answer, all were faced with the "basics of how to *live within* these *very severe restrictions*" [*sic*].

Winki recognized the place of the vulnerable in her life. She witnessed to transforming compassion as she proclaimed that it is always important for her to be with and to know "people who are vulnerable and poor." Her ongoing conversion is noted in her movement from a deep concern and hope for the vulnerable to compassionate commitment to stay with these mothers and children in their struggle to simply survive.

Darlene: Suffering people would influence her view of reality. The volunteers were asked to accompany new refugees in their initial process of immigration and their settlement into the Romero community. Darlene was asked to help Miriam "in her second attempt at claiming refugee status." Miriam arrived back in Toronto after "she was denied and deported three years ago." Darlene reflected on Miriam's smile and the strength of her human spirit:

> I keep thinking of Miriam's eyes and her smile. In her eyes you can see the burden that she carries and the pain that she has suffered and how tired she is of not being settled. But her smile reveals her spirit and strength and grace. I think that the human spirit can endure many things.

As the connection grew between Darlene and Miriam, they became friends. Darlene was "amazed by Miriam's strength and dignity." She was "continually touched by her kindness." In this relationship, Darlene became aware of "how little we have to do to make life so much easier for people in need." She wrote about the blessing of this relationship in her life:

> The time that I have spent with Miriam has been so rewarding for me. I feel that I am doing so little, and she is so gracious and kind. She has welcomed me completely into her life. She has taken me to her home and has fed me. She has given me friendship. When I go to her house, she insists on giving me something, usually tea. Just spending time with her feels like a blessing.

When conversing with Darlene, it was apparent from her thinking and language that she was a theology student:

> This experience helped me to realize that part of living a Christian life is dedicating yourself to others, particularly those in need, because they seem to have an insight into what it means to be a real human being without pretense, without deception.

She knew that her decision to be with disadvantaged people would influence her view of the world and her changing view of reality. She had a deep need for personal "authenticity," and she sensed that she might come to this in an experience of community. She journaled about her choice:

> The decision is being with, working with and caring with [*sic*] those who are oppressed and afraid. In doing this I hope that I will realize more about myself and reality. I keep trying, thinking, feeling, asking questions, listening, hoping, caring, and acting. I don't know what else to do.

Darlene committed herself to the Romero community of refugees, questioning the response of the public and social agencies to the situation of the refugees. Thus she deepened her resolve to be inquiring and responsive. Darlene learned some valuable lessons about the human spirit in the face of adversity:

> It seems that the Christian tradition has been a history of struggle for people to break convention, to change attitudes, and to establish a world of value and decency. In Miriam's case, her determination and hope are consistent with the drive of the human spirit to freedom and to value. The culture is in striking contrast to that drive. This confuses me because it is still a human context. . . . Why is this spirit of freedom and value and love not the primary motivation for these people? I believe that the human spirit is oriented toward truth, freedom, value, love—ultimately God.

Darlene's experience "confirmed" her "understanding that the personal and communal are necessarily linked."

Andrew: A need to contemplate his political activism. When Andrew initially joined the group at Romero House he had an "unacknowledged and unrecognized need to contemplate and discuss [his] political activism." He questioned his involvement in his justice activity: "why . . . and to what end?"

Andrew encountered a homeless man, James, every day, on his way into his office. James was the catalyst for Andrew's changing view of the meaning of justice. While he was inclined to treat James as a "lost cause," when he reflected on his own religious tradition and spirituality, he knew the opposite must be true. He noted, "It is the message of the tradition and spirit that [he] wants to try to respond to and act on."

Andrew's journaling revealed his "spiritual belief that we find God only through our neighbors and the rest of creation—forced [him] to acknowledge and get to know the man [he] passed each day." Through conversations over cups of coffee, Andrew gradually came to know James personally, and to recognize that he was "a child of God." Andrew grew to appreciate the "human goodness" of James.

It was more difficult for Andrew to acknowledge that God might even be within himself. By the end of the first theological reflection process, he had developed to the point where he was able to extend his belief in God's presence to include himself as well as society. With this "intention" in mind, he was able to realize that "grace is somehow intermingled with the sin of society." James, a part of the social reality of the culture "in the position he was in," was a means of "grace" for Andrew.

Mary Jo: Summoned to life. Mary Jo reflected on the power of an incident that called her to deeper trust in the summons of God through the life of another. She considered it "grace" to "hear the command in the voice, in the eyes of another." This occurred for her in the person of a "small child . . . who knew how endangered she was." The child drew a picture to express her unarticulated feelings of fear. This little girl knew "how much she wanted to live" and expressed it in her drawing. Looking at the drawing of a child's smiling face, Mary Jo was moved by her simple but profound caption: "I live!"

Contemplating these words and the vulnerability of the child, Mary Jo experienced a sense of "conversion to the other." In this encounter, she felt "summoned to life." After gazing on this child and her profound but simple drawing, Mary Jo realized that she "would never be the same."

Mary Jo indicated her change from the negative to the positive in her outlook on life and justice. Before coming to Romero House, she saw the "works of justice seemed like an ought." She soon understood, through her relationships with the refugees, that she was "summoned to life." This new life called her to trust in the summons she experienced, and she became a source of "conversion to the other, to hear the command in the voice, in the eyes of another."

The marked change in relationships experienced by the participants was both a sign and an effect of their ongoing process of conversion. Each participant's change in relationship to "the other" became a change in his or her relationship to himself or herself and to God. They moved from simple care to committed concern, from familial relationships to a broader set of relationships, from unanswered academic questions to committed response, from a political critique of problems to attention to the mystery of goodness in oneself, the world, and others. These relationships deepened to become relationships of mercy and compassion.

Ongoing Conversion in Compassionate Service/Works of Mercy

The participants were all initially involved in relationships of service or works of mercy. Compassion appeared to be a primary emotional tone of these relationships, and this sense of mercy held the potential for ongoing conversion in compassionate service.

Shawn: From anger to compassion. From his arrival at Romero House, Shawn's commitment to the brokenness within the lives of the community members and within the community of refugees was evident in his reflection and in his living.

Shawn's compassion was apparent in his daily, faithful relationship with Alireza, one of the refugees. Alireza suffered many years of torture in his homeland, and his story revealed to Shawn the suffering of Christ. Being with the suffering of refugees like Alireza and hearing their stories transformed the anger within Shawn and helped him to struggle with his own experience with his father. In his encounters with the community, he came to know the clarity of his vocation to serve others and to recognize the presence of God in his father's challenge—to be involved in change through service to others.

It became evident that Shawn's anger turned to compassion and trust. He was now "working *for* something or someone, rather than always against an enemy." Shawn's ongoing conversion in the community of compassionate service was recognized in his evolution from working against the brokenness of human systems to working for small faith communities of justice for the reign of God.

> . . . the vision of small faith communities entails a lot of faith (read: trust) [*sic*] trust in the Spirit of God to work through the smallness, the brokenness of the community to produce the realm of God, rather than through the might of human power, wisdom, and agenda, e.g., speck of yeast, small mustard seed—trust in others. This may be even harder, as we need faith in other extremely fallible humans, as God had faith in us.

Shawn envisioned these communities of faith and justice as a new monasticism.

Mary Jo: From soul-destroying stress to compassion. An initial experience for Mary Jo at Romero House was the "simple awareness that [she] liked the people and that they liked [her]," and "being liked" was "most liberating" for her. She realized that "love cannot be an abstraction, a cause . . . but must always be a particular friendship or love of someone who is a refugee."

These relationships "summoned" Mary Jo to love with compassion. She "knew it would mean sharing in [her] neighbors' suffering and anxiety." Although "liberated" and "empowered" by the ethos of the community, she also experienced the ongoing stress caused by the "changes in the immigration system and the political order."

Mary Jo described the anxiety she experienced on behalf of the refugees during an extremely difficult time as being "soul destroying anxiety." Its intensity lasted for a period of "two years." The anxiety was exacerbated "because of the radical uncertainty" about the future of the refugees. For Mary Jo it was the "prospect of their 'arbitrary torture, arrest, imprisonment or death.' It was people [she] knew." In the midst of this tension Mary Jo noted: "I felt I would not give up, and yet I could give up, wear out."

In her reflections she wrote a litany-like notation:

> I hoped my friends would live.
> I wanted the system to change.
> I believed that if we got enough information and worked hard
> enough— then my friends would be accepted.
> I trusted people would listen to them.
> I hoped the people would endure the anxiety and cruelty.
> Me, too.

Mary Jo struggled in her community of compassionate service with a "spirituality of gratitude for all." As she reflected on the anxiety of these times, she said, "I sense that my 'spirituality' of gratitude is appropriate for Romero House but I'm not sure I yet live in a spirit that really embraces the crushing anxiety." She neither wanted to "deny the anxiety" nor let it "define [her] or Romero House." She prayed for the "grace to know how to *be with* anxiety (legitimate anxiety)." At this point she knew that she could be "grateful that the anxiety arises out of care, out of love." She was also deeply aware that she could "only get rid of anxiety at the price of letting go of [her] neighbors." This created an atmosphere of moral discernment for Mary Jo. As she discerned her response, she moved through a process of ongoing conversion from soul-destroying stress and anxiety to compassionate love and gratitude for her life with her neighbors.

Emile: From doing for to being with. Emile came to a new understanding of commitment as he engaged with the community of Romero House. Besides "doing" for others, he learned how important it is "to be there for the other." He noted: "I think it's very important to *be* there for others and not treat them like another case." Emile believed that in working with the poor, the disadvantaged, it was good to "focus on their gifts and what they can offer to others while at the same time being with them through their difficult times."

Emile valued the gifts that individuals brought to community, and he realized that this value was linked to his serious concerns about "our individualistic society." He bridged his beliefs and concerns with his questions: "How to form community? How do we focus on gifts?" His work at Romero House was based on a desire that "people would start to form community and base it on the gifts of each member." In assisting in this process he believed that "people start solving problems by themselves." This individual problem solving enabled members of the community to live life based on their gifts, yet challenged them to care compassionately for each member within the community. It was evident in the leadership Emile demonstrated at Romero House that he was moving his focus from initial anger with the system to supporting gifted individuals as they tried to live within that system—from the state to the human.

The above examples illustrate how relationships were changed and deepened so that the reflectors moved beyond simple human care to a relationship of compassion or mercy. As their relationships became more compassionate, the participants moved, for example, from being against something to considering creative options with others, from abstract concern to compassion for the victim, from anxiety to gratitude, from anger at a system they can't fight to compassion; from a preoccupation with responding to specific external needs to a desire to actualize the internal gifts of others.

Ongoing Conversion to a Deeper Desire for Justice

As the participants reflected on their involvement with the political reality and the effect of their work at Romero House on their spiritual lives, threads of ongoing conversion were evident in their journals and dialogue. The movement from fear and anger to courage and witness in the political forum was obvious. As they reported on personal and communal changes, they noted the wisdom and inspiration they received from Scripture. A strong desire to bring about the reign of God and to know the presence of God at work in their political encounters was noticeable in their journaling.

Shawn: Seeking courage from the prophets and the gospel. As Shawn tried to reevaluate his political commitments, he experienced a movement from "fear" to "seeking courage from the prophets and the gospel." Although a young man, he knew himself as "politically conscious for at least the last five years." During those years he "supported the political left and trusted the idea of a strong social net to secure justice." During this time, he was challenged through a conversation to consider that "the traditional political . . . left had lost its voice for justice" and was no longer a "viable means of bringing about the Kingdom of God." He began to realize that his political "thinking was quite entrenched and doctrinal." He sensed that he was "afraid to give up his 'faith' in his political model."

After reflecting on this challenge and the question of how the church and the state relate, he came to this resolve:

> We will still shout our challenge, both to the right *and* the left. But we must move "beyond the social gospel" to a new level of *faith in action.* The leaven of our hope, and God's hope will be the catalyst of a political conversion of the "powers that be" and not the other way around.

Shawn displayed the enthusiasm of a young, politically active person and the fervor of a new convert to Christianity. He demonstrated openness in his willingness to receive a challenge, reflect on it, and realize a new vision. He believed that "God transforms the world not by forcing the world . . . but rather by the faith of the 'elect'—the small ones." He believed in the Scripture saying: "Only a few grains of yeast will make the bread rise."

Darlene: From achieving to being. As a theology student, Darlene wondered how to make the world in which she lived more human, and she associated this with a sense of compassion. Darlene believed that "it is feeling that motivates." She sensed a "tremendous compassion for those who are afraid and desperate." Her relationship with Miriam put her in touch with these feelings. It was Miriam's smile at Darlene when they were in the immigration office that touched and challenged Darlene. It was Miriam's simple cup of tea, offered in friendship, which led her to strong feelings of compassion and to ask the question: "Were not our hearts on fire?"

In this question and in deeper insight, Darlene knew that she was changing. She believed that she was in the process of conversion as a result of her move toward "the reality of the oppressed." Darlene acknowledged that Miriam "has been my teacher in this experience." From this relationship Darlene learned that conversion is more about being than achieving. She understood that "conversion is something I have to give myself over to. I have to let go of the notion of who I am and what I have to do in order to be happy, good, secure, and who I have to be." Her movement from compassion to service evolved into an appreciation for her conversion.

Elizabeth: From doubtful thoughts to hopeful relationships. When Elizabeth first came to Romero House, the issue of canceling legal aid services for refugees was being deliberated at Osgoode Hall, the seat of Toronto's legal system. She "knew deep down" that she would never be in need of this kind of legal aid, but she felt the "desperation" of the people with whom she now lived, and Elizabeth "could not figure out why [she] felt this way."

Upon reflection, she came to understand that her "personal relationships with the refugees at Romero House were why [she] felt so angry and afraid." She recognized that a number of political causes affected the overall feeling of anxiety: the government's financial cut from the welfare program; the tax break rebate, especially for the wealthy; and her perception of a "wave of conservatism sweeping the land that cultivates a feeling of 'having to tighten our belts.'"

Elizabeth believed that this growth in conservatism "cultivates a need for personal development and fulfillment rather than communal development." She, however, believed that community is the key to justice and that "when we deal with people on an equal level as fellow human beings . . . we build community."

Elizabeth saw the food bank as a place of struggle, which held little possibility for hope. The 21 percent cuts to welfare forced a deluge of people, mostly women, to resort to food banks as a normal way to obtain what they needed to feed their families.

> I hated the food bank. What a horrible, degrading place (the
> atmosphere of the place makes you feel guilty for being poor).
> I wished it just looked and smelled better. I wished none of
> these people needed the food bank.

Elizabeth wondered how this situation might be improved. Her question reflected one seeking hope for systemic change, "How could this place be made differently? I doubted things would be better in the future." Note that her creative question of hope was quickly followed by a statement of negativity and doubt.

Experiencing "this kind of desperation and fear" at the food bank, Elizabeth reflected on the experience of poor persons. Her abiding question was, "How did these people (waiting for food) feel about what was going on?" Elizabeth had no answer to her query, but she continued to think positively and wanted to accompany the refugee women in the midst of their struggle and fear.

As a young volunteer, Elizabeth was disillusioned by the raw reality of poverty she encountered at the food bank. She found herself fighting an inadequate system, trying to respond in some positive way to the financial cutbacks in government programs. Although Elizabeth had thoughtful, hopeful questions and suggestions about changing the system, she continued to struggle with a seemingly futile system. Placing her hope in the women rather than in the system helped to move Elizabeth from doubts to hope, from bureaucratic dysfunction to personal relationship.

Elizabeth credits her negative visits to the food bank for giving her "insight into how life should be" in a more just society. She wanted and needed to contribute to this reality. "The experience at the food bank affirms the fact that people should be treated with respect and dignity, and as people. . . . When we connect, we build community."

Elizabeth "felt challenged by this experience." She questioned it in the light of her faith. "What could God possibly have in store for us with this crisis?" This questioning was "not a negative thing" for Elizabeth. In fact, she "felt a sense of hope," which turned to confidence that the community would "survive this crisis." It also held an "affirmation" and a "call." Elizabeth reflected:

I knew we would make it through and I knew something good would come out of it. It was during this experience that I really felt affirmed. This is what I am meant to be doing. To fight for justice, to be with those in need. I really felt my calling . . . It was pretty exhilarating.

Andrew: A world in the process of being redeemed. Committed to social reform, Andrew moved from viewing the "sociopolitical context as largely negative" to seeking the presence of God in the midst of it. He came to realize that his initially negative view emerged from a culture that "told [him] to ignore James [his homeless friend] as a lost cause." Andrew's process of ongoing conversion was evident—move from viewing society as sinful to seeking the signs of God in both the darkness and the light of today's society, and even in himself. Where once he saw only a fallen world, he now saw a world in a process of being, with hope for its redemption. With a sense of God's presence, he continued to work for political reform.

Mary Jo: A heightened critique of systems. Mary Jo's involvement with refugees heightened her critique of the systems involved in government services. In her opinion, "refugees have become the symbol of global upheaval—and seem to be the focus of efforts to control the recession and consequent insecurities." She knew that usually tolerant people become intolerant "in times of economic and social stress," and there is an "attempt to wall out the rest of the world . . . as national borders are being erased through global economic forces." As these forces grow in strength, "people feel an increased need to 'control' the boundaries of the country."

Mary Jo experienced discipleship in the Gospel call to love of neighbor in the context of the "decline of the West." Love of neighbor "has become more difficult than [she] could ever have imagined because of changes in the immigration system and the political order."

Emile: The hope of people helping people. Emile evolved from feeling anger toward the government to witnessing publicly to his beliefs about politics and community. Initially, he expressed strong feelings of "anger toward the cutbacks" imposed by the government.

His main complaint was that "there has been no transition time" for those in need. In his journal he wrote:

> Governments everywhere are abandoning their role as social service providers. And since people have been used to this for such a long time they presently don't know what to do. This is difficult and will force more people to come together.

Emile was inspired by a group of people that provided time and hope in this transition: "the people that received a tax break and were willing to give that up so that the poor could benefit and be helped out." This news gave Emile "a feeling of wonderment and awe." Emile described these persons as "real"—"that makes a difference. People helping people."

"Hands held out towards each other" was the symbol for Emile to begin to have hope in the "rich seeing the injustice." He also hoped in his efforts to enable a "community of gifts in spite of brokenness." Fewer people would experience being treated "like numbers by the government," or fall through the cracks in the system.

Emile's political belief was strengthened by his faith that "Jesus calls us to community in our brokenness." This belief was witnessed to by Emile as he moved from prayer to action in his political involvement. He publicly spoke to the federal committee on finance regarding the current cutbacks in services and welfare. In this change from anger with the government to engaging politicians and the rich, he based his speech on his meditation and beliefs in the value and dignity of the human person.

Winki: The power of cooperative communities. Winki is in a life-long process of developing from someone who lives simply to someone who commits herself to seeing that others may simply live. She lives what she thinks and wastes few words talking about it. Winki noted a number of times in her reflections her strong philosophical and Christian belief in the statement: "Live simply in order for others to simply live."

Winki questioned how the Gospel mandate can be lived: "How will the poor be housed, clothed and fed?" The "current political and economic situation" continued to challenge her. How could she help to transform conditions of poverty? She lived simply. She responded to the Gospel through works of mercy. It was evident that Winki's understanding of living was being transformed.

Winki sought hope by creating a simple "focus group" of Romero House women to discuss their needs, and in facilitating it she was "both challenged and confirmed." As time passed, the Women's Group gained great significance in the lives of these refugees. Winki used a capital *S* when she described and redefined the reality of this group: "it has evolved culturally to be a Sustaining group." It was a place of hope for the women of Romero where they could respond to their family, health, and social concerns. Winki began the group to help the members function better in their new surroundings.

Winki shared in the hope of this life-sustaining group in the midst of serious struggle. One of the refugees in particular inspired Winki. "She never seemed to doubt that God is Good." In recognizing the deep hope this woman had in a good God, Winki was challenged to ongoing conversion. It deepened her realization of the strength of the Christian tradition and the power of cooperative communities. She moved from a strong belief in living simply to a deeper understanding of injustice and the call to justice.

Darlene: Service foundational to the study of theology. It was "shocking" for Darlene to come to know and to try to help Miriam and "to realize her beauty in light of the coldness and inhumanity of the social system." In her journal she wrote:

> I took her to get her welfare. I was in the room with her. She was noticeably tired and strained, but she smiled at me and trusted me to be with her. I keep thinking, why do these people have to suffer so much? The welfare worker was mechanical and distant. How do we keep the humanity in all of this?"

She explicitly referred to "conversion" as she reflected on her commitment to move to the Romero House community.

> I really don't think that complete (if that ever happens) conversion is possible if the person is isolated from the reality of the

oppressed. I had to move from the judgment of value (what is good) to the decision to act on that judgment by living and working with these people. If you don't follow through with that process the conversion cannot be complete because you're not allowing yourself to be affected.

Darlene became committed to learning "what to do" and "what to do together" to create a better world. For Darlene, caring for others was a way to be human. Darlene also realized how "foundational" her service to others was to her study of theology, as she began "living and working with those who are oppressed and exploited."

Andrew: A movement toward communities of care. Andrew frequently referred to communities of solidarity and care. In his professional work as an advocate for justice, solidarity was a high value. He had made a "life commitment . . . to work for the community . . . rooted in a worldview of mutual dependence." He noted that his "spirituality is rooted in community or solidarity." He hoped that communities of care will replace the need for the politics of advocacy.

Andrew responded to the invitation to reflect with the Romero community because "it is a community of solidarity with those who have little power in society." Here he "hoped to witness and benefit from the witness of others around the table." In reflecting on this time in history and the context of ministry, Andrew indicated that "this culture has so many people freely alienated/marginalized, disconnected and alone that there is a profound need for community." Andrew noted his hope that "new communities of care will rise up (out of necessity) to replace broken democracy." He has a strong conviction that

> the cutbacks in Ontario are part of a global movement of rapid competition for material gain; there is fear that there isn't enough for everyone anymore, so we've gotta take whatever we can.

Andrew was persuaded that the financial cutbacks to "community agencies and voluntary organizations" contained a "paradox." At the very time when communities are being undermined by a pervasive spirit and culture of individualism . . . the cutbacks will make the inequality of our society so apparent that Ontarians will come to their senses, remember compassion and extend it and demand it. . . . I sense a movement toward community, communal care as the only possible, positive response.

Through their relationships, the participants had moved from seeing "the other" to relating with them as neighbors and friends. Within this deepening relationship of compassion and mercy, they also became more merciful toward themselves; they moved to a deeper and more positive desire for justice; from an ideology of justice to a biblical view of justice; from judgment to decisions; from addressing needs to integrating faith and justice; from seeing the world as fallen to seeing it as in the process of redemption; from seeing the country through middle-class eyes to seeing it from the margins; from prayer to action; from seeing enemies to seeking allies among the rich and politicians; from mercy to justice.

Ongoing Conversion to Christian Love

It was a revelation of the mystery of ongoing conversion to see the group at Romero House move from mercy to justice to Christian love.

Darlene: Vulnerability reveals the light. During the weeks of this reflection period, Darlene's faith gradually moved from a place of darkness to a place of light. The Amnesty International symbol, a candle entwined with barbed wire, became her image of this transformation. For Darlene the light of faith was frequently "a light sustaining itself under pressure, pain."

Darlene was inspired by the staff and their reflections on the gospels. From some of the staff she felt a call to live in "simplicity"; from others, a call to "become like little children." A significant kindness Darlene experienced was from Miriam, a woman whose vulnerability revealed the potential of the human spirit. Her relationship with Miriam broke through Darlene's darkness and released light to her spirit. She continued to be aware of the dignity and strength in Miriam's smile. This gave Darlene confidence in the human spirit. It gave her the grace to know her own capacity to endure pain and to accompany others in their vulnerable experiences of life.

Darlene noted that Miriam was "a very hopeful person" and was "confident in maintaining a position that humans are basically good and loving." However, being in touch with the pain experienced by some of the refugees caused Darlene to question her capacity for joy and hope in the midst of the ministry of Romero House. "My doubts are concerning my own capacity to remain happy, to become joyous in the face of this. Pain strikes a very deep chord with me."

She desired to live in "honesty, curiosity, love, and laughter." She often asked herself the question the disciples asked: "Were not our hearts on fire?" Her reflections were mixed and she often "felt very far away from God." This was "terrifying." At the same time Darlene felt "profoundly compassionate." She was aware of an "inconsistency" and "confusion" in her thoughts and feelings. She noted: "I believe in God but I don't feel God. . . . Something motivates me to continue trying though. That feels like more than me."

At the end of the reflection period, Darlene sensed both the "presence of injustice and the light against injustice." She acknowledged the "continual presence of God's love in hardship and in joy." In herself she felt the "call and need for continual conversion of heart, mind (and spirit)." At the validation meeting, Darlene was able to say: "I am secure in my faith. My struggle still lies in living out my faith in the face of fears and insecurities. Being with our reflection group has helped to lessen the fears."

Darlene seemed to have moved from a place of suspicion to a place of friendship and love. There was a new sense of joy in Darlene's capacity to express herself and reach out to others in this community of care.

Mary Jo: How can we see the face of God again? It was apparent that through a process of ongoing conversion, Mary Jo moved from simple reflection and critical analysis to a deeper Christian commitment by reflecting on the gospels and contemplative love. Her scriptural reflections led her to believe that "the reach of Jesus" extends "mercy" into life and society. From her cultural analysis she believed that violence "must be resisted at a profound level of Spirit." From this critical and contemplative stance she hoped to live a life of Christian discipleship.

In facing the violence of society, and from working at Romero House, Mary Jo raised the question: "How have the poor become so defaced?" She also asked a new question: "How can we see their face and the face of God again?" For Mary Jo, the answer to these questions, her commitment to justice, and the Gospel mandate of "love of neighbor," came from living with refugees. She noted on her journal sheet: "I discovered that you will be happy if you hunger and thirst for justice, because you love your neighbor."

Mary Jo realized that there was a great "happiness in gospel living that the world cannot give." She believed that, with the scriptural imperative to "love our neighbors," we are given the grace of response. She journaled:

> Love your neighbor—is a command which carries with it
>   the grace of response.
> You will be happy if you are poor in spirit.
> You will be happy if you desire one thing.
> You will be happy if you hunger and thirst for justice.

Mary Jo did not expect that she "would enjoy so much" living and working with the refugees as "neighbors." She soon found that "it was as if the gospel was alive at every moment." From what I observed, this movement from love, to stress, to thirst for justice, to Gospel joy, created deeper integration in Mary Jo. Her reflections revealed that she was open to the ongoing conversion of loving her neighbors, and graced with the fruit of happiness arising from these relationships.

Mary Jo understood that her "primary experience of God" was the "realization that life itself, just being, is a gift, a miracle, and that the only spirituality that fits for [her] is one of gratitude." Through prayer and meditation she knew that this spirituality was appropriate, even in the "crushing anxiety" of these times.

Mary Jo's spirituality of gratitude called her to "reach out" and "trust":

> [I]t is the reach of Justice and Mercy—as when Jesus reached out and said, "of course I want to help you." TRUST that Jesus is already reaching to help these people. A reach that cannot be forever blocked by systems.

To learn to reach out as Jesus did required a new way of being for Mary Jo. She realized that for her to live the Gospel she needed to live from a "contemplative" stance:

> I feel the need to be immersed in a sense of God's love (contemplative) because there is profound violence in what is happening. This must be resisted at a profound level of Spirit.

Mary Jo's faith moved from the "ought" of justice to a lived conviction of the Gospel commitment to love. Her Gospel spirituality of gratitude and dependence on God was seen in her life and reflections: "Go with what is given—through others, from God." In her search for a way to do justice in the midst of violence and anxiety, Mary Jo looks to Jesus. "Perhaps it is the reach of Justice and Mercy—as when Jesus reached out and said: 'Of course I want to help you.'"

Mary Jo's ongoing conversion in Christian discipleship was exemplified in a simple movement from being liked to a profound commitment to love of neighbor. Through this process she moved from scriptural reflections and cultural analysis to a "deepening desire to be a follower of Jesus—again—with the kind of simplicity [she] had in the earlier days of [her] commitment."

Emile: If we are free enough to follow him, we can be at home everywhere. Emile described his "faith vision" as a "life of service." His motivating questions were: "How do I find God in others?" "How do I bring about God's Kingdom through others?" He came to believe that "God works beyond our narrow scope of religion."

An important aspect of Emile's faith was prayer. He believed that in prayer he was able to be in touch with himself and with the Spirit of God. He noted: "To pray in silence, to be silent, you can really get in touch with what is going on inside yourself. You're better able to hear what God wants to communicate to you."

Through the prayerful discernment of his life's vocation, Emile recognized a new depth of spirituality. He wrote: "My experience, which called me into a life of more direct service with the poor, and to do it communally, has deepened my spirituality." Emile did not doubt that his current experience of community and service was "more intense" than any of his past experiences. He credited his faith with helping him to feel "at home" in his new experience, for he believed that "God brings us where He wants and if we are free enough to follow Him, we can feel at home anywhere with others whom we had not known."

Winki: God is personal in everyone. As Winki contemplated Senait and her children, she noticed "the Christian parallel of Mary and Joseph's flight as refugees, with a small child at risk, willing to be refugees in order to save the life of their child." She was inspired as she realized that the woman "prayed to God daily" and was a "tremendous witness—of faith." Winki knew that this courageous woman and others like her were a reflection of God, and so she asked: "Does anyone know how close they were to God? Do we know the face of God in them?"

Winki's reflections on Senait revealed a memory of a previous moment of conversion at the St. George Street subway station, in downtown Toronto, in the midst of the comings and goings of daily commuters. At that time she was conscious of her deep anger toward Christianity but in that instant she realized that "religion is not in the practice of Christianity but religion is about faith in God." She knew that if she accepted faith, she could know God. Winki desired to know God and realized that faith is about God and about living "as Jesus did." The summons from this vision of faith for Winki was to believe that "God is present in everyone." She knew as she stood at the subway stop that she was challenged in discipleship to "welcome the stranger as Jesus did. . . . To be open to respond to the 'call' of the Spirit at a very simple level . . . Meeting people in an atmosphere of tolerance and welcome."

Winki was "moved" and "witnessed" to by "the great faith and determination of Senait." She acknowledged how this refugee woman "came to a new place and was open to her neighbors." This relationship enabled Winki to believe strongly that "human dignity brings us face to face with the image of God in our friends who are struggling within their poverty." This new relationship called her to continue to live as Jesus did.

Andrew: A call from God. In his reflections, Andrew expressed his belief that "grace is central to the Christian tradition." He knew that the current welfare cutbacks "are a rejection of some of the central Christian tenets and values." He understood welfare as "the safety net intended to be on behalf of the community." By cutting this safety net, Andrew believed the government was rejecting "the scriptural injunction to 'break the yoke of the oppressed, plead the cause of the widow, care for the orphan'. . ."

He hoped for a more "perfect world" in which "the call of God would carry more weight than the call of the state." Until then Andrew sensed the need to "redefine communities; not pit them against each other." He saw "communities of care" as "spirit-induced". . . "allowing grace free and full expression."

Andrew was politically conscious and socially active for years. His desire was to become more conscious of God's presence in the very situations of his "social policy and work/activism." Andrew's need for hope in his vocational call was evident in the following statement: "My doubt was that I was not 'called' to this work at all but that it was chance and nothing more that brought me to it."

After reflecting with the study group for over two years and participating in this theological reflection process, Andrew grew to recognize his life of service as a call from God. He journaled about being challenged and confirmed in his sense of call through these reflections. His notes reveal hope and an acceptance of his experience of service through "glimpses of God's role" in his life. Andrew's religious and political experience became more interrelated:

> I have gained some glimpses of God's role in bringing me to where I was/am. I've grown somewhat more comfortable ac-

cepting that I was indeed called to work for justice and to live
a life of service.

Andrew confronted his self-doubt and accepted his call through
noticing God's role in his life. It was clear that this happened as he
engaged with a community of faith and study:

> I've come to recognize the truth of the journey, and the fact
> that the journey (spiritual) is enough. I feel God's motivation
> and pricking of conscience in bringing me to seek answers to
> these questions in the first place.

During this time Andrew "gained some glimpses of God's role"
in bringing him to where he is today. Andrew considered this experience a

> backwards kind of conversion . . . trying to uncover or discern
> something in [his] life that [he] believed was already there: a
> call to community with like-minded traditions as "witness."

Elizabeth: Loving your neighbor as yourself. In witnessing the
struggle of the people at the food bank, Elizabeth became more convinced of the dignity of the human person and the need to build
community in an atmosphere of respect. She relied on her vision of
Christianity and conversion that we are called to love our neighbor:

> For me Christianity is very basic. It deals with people face to
> face—it looks at their whole being and affirms it. . . . What is
> needed is a link or contact between individuals. I think "loving
> your neighbor as yourself" ideally fulfills my conception of
> Christianity. Conversion is needed. Conversion to humanness
> is needed.

Elizabeth trusted in community as an alternative and a moral imperative. It offers a fellowship where people can be treated with
dignity and be connected, can live and work together as family. She
wants to "build community" by being a "good neighbor." In her
journal she noted: "If everyone began to see others as human we
could *connect*. When we connect we can build community. At least
community can be built."

Elizabeth's powerful trust in connectedness was founded on her "love of neighbor" as epitomized in the refugee women. She also believed in "the spirit of God at work" in these women, and in her insight into "social justice as part of her faith vision." From a sense of powerlessness, Elizabeth was "challenged and called" to live a life of social justice. She trusted in the prophetic power of building "community," connecting with others for "human rights," and the Spirit of God at work in our lives.

Shawn: Beyond an agenda; a vision. Previous to this reflection process, the Romero community decided to have a prayer vigil at Osgoode Hall, the seat and symbol of legal services in Ontario. The vigil was envisioned as a way of drawing to the attention of those voting on the legal aid issue the seriousness of the situation and the ramifications of any cutbacks. It was a way to seek spiritual strength for the difficult days ahead if the vote ended up in favor of the cutbacks. The vigil was a twenty-four-hour prayer service in which the staff was joined by refugees and friends of Romero House. Shawn saw the vigil as "a small group of Christians bearing witness."

It was a way of "standing up and being counted," a call to "witness against the powers that be." He experienced a desire to "trust that God would speak a word" to him during this time of prayer. His feelings were "interspersed with anger, joy, good humor, and as always, a wee touch of melancholy."

The image of the prophet was a powerful one for Shawn. It came up several times in the Scripture readings and "reminded [him] of the strength and power" of the prophetic tradition. At the same time it revealed the truth of the "often hidden . . . fatigue" of the figure of the prophet.

His experience included the contrast of "darkness and light, many new faces, and physically being confronted (briefly) with 'the enemy,' the lawyers." It clarified his previous experience of "legal aid as a sort of vague abstract issue controlled by faceless forces." It became a "concrete, real, flesh and blood experience . . ." in which he was "personally involved."

Shawn felt both "excitement and lethargy" at the vigil. His excitement kept him motivated, but he also felt tired and powerless.

As Scriptures were read and as he prayed through the night, he was inspired by the words of the prophets. He felt connected to "the fatigue within the prophetic tradition, which is often hidden by the strength and power of the prophet's stories."

As the vigil progressed, he sensed the inspiration and witness of the prophets of the past. He wondered about the prophetic role of the church as a witness to the current government. Shawn's burning questions were as follows: "How does the church relate to the state?" and, "Can the government be converted as we challenge its power . . . with the message of the gospel?"

As Shawn did not arrive at a specific answer to these questions during the vigil, he returned to them during the theological reflection process. He also brought to this reflection some of his readings, questions, and insights from a class he was attending on theology and culture. He reflected that, in the churches and in politics, there has been a "loss of power" of the "political left" as a "voice of justice." He "realized that the traditional political left is no longer seen as a viable means of bringing about the Kingdom of God."

During the vigil, Shawn wanted to "rely on God's strength" but "just didn't know quite how." He realized that "faith to do this is a gift":

> So during the Vigil, I found that, though we were just watching and waiting, it was an active watching and waiting, not passive. This is real, a microcosm of the way I do my work and live out my vision, action. However, the danger is that when my work is seen as mine rather than a gift from God, vision becomes agenda, and I soon start running on ice, burning out. I need to remember that it is God working . . .

Through this reflection process Shawn began to trust that his fatigue and powerlessness connected him to the fragile power of the prophets. He realized that his presence at the vigil on behalf of the refugees and his encounters with the lawyers made the issues of his concern a reality for others.

Shawn grew to appreciate the gift of faith and how it contributed to his works of justice on behalf of others. At the legal aid vigil, he prayed for the gift to see his work as God's work, and he continues to do so as he reflects on this experience. He ended his reflection with a new trust in the prophetic power of grace. "Activity is only fruitful and faithful when it is a manifestation of God's active grace."

It is gratifying to see the rich threads of ongoing conversion from compassionate service to Christian love. In many instances, experiences of darkness moved into light. Struggle against the political and social systems in place moved to hope as the situation was met with prophetic wisdom, Gospel spirituality, and commitment to Christian community. Several of the reflective participants moved from skepticism and critical analysis to the profound simplicity of Gospel love of neighbor.

In summary, it seemed evident that the theological reflection process allowed the participants to enter new relationships with "the other" and by doing so became transformed or their relationships converted into relationships of mercy and justice. Ultimately, this led them more deeply into the mystery of Christian Love, its blessing and burden, its joy and great suffering. Through a deeper conversion to the meaning of love, they came to believe in themselves and God in a different way.

A RITUAL OF COMPASSION

As a closing active response to the theological reflection process, the group decided to process prayerfully around Queen's Park, the government buildings of the Province. They chose to have a member lead them carrying a cross as a symbol of the crucified poor. This was their political response in faith to a 21 percent cutback in welfare. The cutbacks greatly affected not just the refugees of the Romero House community but the poor and disadvantaged of Ontario.

In the Queen's Park vigil, the final ritual of the group, the cross took on great importance as an icon of the experience. It was carried at times by friends of Romero House, students and staff from Regis College and the Toronto School of Theology, persons from the Toronto area committed to justice, and friends from Buffalo who work with refugees at the Canada–United States border.

When the refugees took their turns carrying the cross, I was deeply moved, as some of them were Muslim or of no formal religious persuasion. It was inspiring to witness their respect for the Christian tradition, their interfaith wisdom, and their simplicity of heart and purpose. They witnessed to me a freedom to participate in a religious activity that held no boundary or border for them, except what Mary Jo Leddy, one of the participants, would name "The Border Called Hope."[6]

CONCLUSION

In guiding this process I observed the participants reflecting on their initial connections to Romero House and their experiences of assisting refugees settling into Toronto. Many of the participants' reflections were ones of faith and struggle to make meaning of the circumstances and the sufferings experienced by their new neighbors, the refugees. They were critically aware of the political systems surrounding them and how this had an impact on the lives of the refugees. To see God in this experience was both a challenge and a grace for the participants. In the end, some knew God in the crucifixion of the refugees and some knew Mystery in their own experience of compassion for the other. Many were moved to hope in the contagious courage of the refugees as they faced their forced exile, trusting in a better future for their children.

My deepest feelings during this process were empathy and shared hope. I felt for and with the participants as they reflected on their experiences and struggled in faith with the meaning of it all. They sought ways to respond to the daily situations of stress that confronted them, especially to a political system that was originally designed to be of service to the refugees and for the poor. I experienced deep hope that they might respond with the courage they absorbed from their relationships with the refugees and from the compassion, which rose from their own depths.

Chapter 4

EXPLORING THE CONTEXT

❖

The second step in theological reflection is an analysis of the contextual reality of the experience. This involves rational and intuitive questions concerning such matters as the history, the cultural background, or the socioeconomic values of those who are burdened and those who benefit in a particular context. Themes and symbols may become evident at this phase of the process. This part of the reflection results in assumptions being confirmed, disconfirmed, or transformed in light of new insights. Fostering an awareness of the context of experiences allows the person to realize the importance of reflective analysis.

There are two overlapping contexts that situate the reality of this ministerial experience: (1) globalization and its impact on refugees, and the marginalized; and (2) the dominant culture of North America and its manifestation in "The Common Sense Revolution" of Ontario, Canada.

In understanding the context of this study, I am deeply concerned about who benefits and who is burdened as a consequence of paying attention to these realities.

GLOBALIZATION

Globalization is the term generally used to describe a new world order that is exceedingly complex and rapidly changing. It can be defined as the "compression of time and space and integration of features of society brought about by advances in communication and transportation technologies."[1] This movement began as a result of the political alignments following the Cold War and continues with new but often uncertain political arrangements today. However, many nations are also still seeking, although with new caution, financially viable relationships that have grown through the 1990s and into the millennium. Computerization, beginning in the 1980s and affecting all forms of communication, contributed greatly to the speed of this interconnectedness, and helped to make the world a smaller place. New technologies are now enhancing the global flow of information as well as supporting the movement of goods, services, and peoples.

The implications of such rapid change, the ethical questions arising as a result of these advances in all aspects of our lives, and the effect of these changes on the economic well-being of the poor compel us, as we continue into this twenty-first century, to ponder the forms of solidarity needed to hold together the more fragile communities within society. Romero House is one such haven—a movement or spirituality of solidarity.

Robert Schreiter, in a lecture given in Edmonton, Alberta, named the age of globalization a "New Modernity" and questioned how we are to live and believe in such an "unstable world."[2] In this traumatic environment, North America, particularly the United States, struggles to move ahead financially despite severe competition and flux in the world market. As the demands of globalization escalate and personal and societal relationships suffer along the way, we are encouraged to imagine a more just alternative and humane approach with the slogan "Another world is possible."[3] It is just such another world that the Romero House community is creating in a west-end neighborhood of Toronto.

As globalization moves into another decade, many feel powerless in face of a process that seems "inevitable." However, an alternative vision is seen in the growing awareness of those on the margins of society. Concern for less developed nations is also growing, as the negative impact of this movement is experienced among the impoverished of the world. New initiatives among socially responsible economists give hope that there are now creative ways to share global resources more equitably and curb the excesses of globalization.[4] The shared garden of the Romero House community, a dream of this reflection group, is an initiative created to share the local resource of food in a local neighborhood setting. These global and local initiatives challenge the temptation to accept the inevitable powerlessness globalization engenders.

The Migration of Peoples

A significant sign of globalization is the increasing migration of peoples throughout the world. (Such movements, of course, have taken place over the centuries. For example, the people of Israel were warned by God, through Moses, not to wrong or oppress aliens and strangers, reminding them that they were once aliens in the land of Egypt [Exod 22:21-22].) The United Nations Development Program's 2004 report on migration "estimates that at this point in history one out of every thirty-five persons on the planet is a migrant."[5] When someone seeking shelter knocks on the door of Romero House, they represent one of these statistics. As they settle into this setting they become a neighbor to other migrating persons in this community. It is a wonder to behold, as in some cases onetime tribal enemies now share the same space and services.

This migration is seen not only across continents but is also seen within continents. Currently Africa is experiencing this growing phenomenon between and within countries, especially around large cities such as Lagos, Nigeria, the world's sixth largest city. "Across Africa, as millions of rural residents migrate to cities in search of jobs, the cost of urban land is going up, infrastructure is inadequate and authoritarian regimes are using forced evictions to manage the problem."[6] The burden of this epic movement is on individuals as well as societies and governments. The social and psychological problems of migration cause great turbulence in our contemporary world as people search for a better life elsewhere or are driven by the forces of poverty and war.

Globalization and the migration of peoples have changed the neighborhoods of the major cities of the world. Toronto and Vancouver are now considered the two cities in the world with the highest percentages and varieties of ethnic backgrounds.[7] This trend is expected to continue as long as people suffer from economic and political instability.

There are growing tensions against immigration in countries that were traditionally open to the migration of peoples. This raises the question: How much diversity can a stable society sustain? Great Britain, a country traditionally open to others, has recently turned against asylum seekers. Other countries now say they are "full" and cannot accept any more "foreigners." On the other hand, migrants are needed to provide the labor necessary to maintain a now expected given standard of living in many first-world countries.[8] These tensions will continue to escalate as the migration of peoples continues to increase, a serious call to create urban communities that will promote new patterns of cultural interaction in multicultural settings. It is remarkable to me that such a dynamic vision of engaging small groups of multicultural communities is fostered by the staff and volunteers of the Romero House community in their Toronto neighborhood.

As this millennium evolves we find ourselves in a more unstable time than when globalization began at the end of the Cold War, or with the fall of the Berlin Wall in 1989. The growing reality and threat of global terrorism is a major concern throughout the world. Earth-shattering natural disasters and dramatic climate changes are creating a new consciousness of the fragility of our planet.

In times of instability and crisis, people are much less able to tolerate ambiguity or respond to creative challenges. For example, the challenge of accepting a multicultural world was significantly altered in North America following the events of September 11, 2001. "In times of risk, an openness to the different and the unknown becomes simply too dangerous."[9] A result of this growing intolerance is the scapegoating of refugees by some members of society who once considered them positive symbols of globalization.

Migrating peoples and mixed cultural communities are a real challenge in our unstable world. Migrants strive for strategic ways to live in new and unfamiliar cultures amid both welcoming and hostile neighbors. As Schreiter sums up this reality, he notes that we are challenged to "live together in the shrunken space and time of globalization, in the convergence of peoples in migration, amid new ways of living and believing in an unstable world." [10] He seeks the wisdom of St. Paul to remind us that we are called to live together as a global community in local neighborhoods: "[N]o longer strangers and aliens, but . . . citizens . . . of the household of God . . ." (Eph 2:19). The spirit of this Scripture was alive in my experience of the participants of this study as they made friends with the refugees at Romero House and looked on them as new neighbors rather than as threatening strangers.

The World of the Refugee

Refugees have always faced a unique risk and challenge in the migration of peoples. Following World War II and the catastrophe of the Holocaust, the Western world had to acknowledge its refusal to deal with global refugees. In light of this tragedy, a United Nations Convention on the Status of Refugees held in Geneva, Switzerland, in 1951, defined the term "refugee" as a person who,

> owing to a well-founded fear of being persecuted for reasons of race, religion, nationality, membership of a particular social group, or political opinion, is outside the country of his nationality, and is unable to or, owing to such fear, is unwilling to avail himself of the protection of that country . . . [11]

This definition applies even more strongly today.

The convention also obliged the host country to protect refugees facing possible persecution in their country of origin. This places a moral obligation on all countries to support the movement of refugees throughout our world. At the dawn of the twenty-first century, the number of unsettled refugees and asylum seekers in the world is a massive 37.4 million (United Nations High Commissioner for

Refugees, UNHCR, June 2008). Refugee migration affects the entire global community as they move about within their countries of origin, or wait at sites along the journey for final destinations, or seek refuge at asylums scattered throughout the world. Canada, as a signatory of this convention, has agreed to offer assistance and protection to refugees, as it can. Romero House is one such haven for the homeless refugee who often, through a variety of dangerous circumstances, arrives on its doorstep.

Over 140 nation-states are committed to protecting refugees through various international agreements. It is estimated that the more developed countries have absorbed over 40 percent of the global refugees. However, some African and Asian nations often host even larger numbers, and more than two-thirds of all refugees are hosted by nations with a per capita income of less than $2,000.[12]

A current example of the tightening control around the migration of peoples is the 2002 Safe Third Country Accord signed by Canada and the United States.[13] This accord forces all refugees seeking asylum in Canada to apply in the United States first if they stop there on their way to Canada, and vice versa. In the past, almost 35 percent of refugees came to Canada through the US. This new regulation will delay and even hinder refugees from reaching their final destination.[14]

This law has caused a real concern among social justice and human rights communities, both civil and religious, who feel that refugees are becoming the new scapegoats of heightened security programs throughout our world, especially in North America. However, Schreiter notes hopefully that this turmoil is causing people striving for justice to ache for peace and freedom. He believes that "social conflicts that have uprooted more than a hundred million people worldwide to create ongoing camps of displaced persons and flows of refugees into other countries has made people yearn for peace and repair from such disastrous occurrences."[15] Such yearning was voiced in the reflection and prayer of the participants of this study.

Refugees are only one aspect of this global migration of peoples. In Canada almost 12 percent of landed immigrants are refugees.

Although Canada's official acceptance of refugees is considered one of the highest in the West, if a person is refused status as a refugee under the Geneva Convention regulations, there is no alternative for them and they face deportation, unlike some European countries that enable about 80 percent of refugees rejected as conventional refugees to stay under some other arrangement.[16] Accompanying resident refugees back to the border for deportation is one of the most disheartening tasks the Romero House staff has to perform.

Fleeing refugees, many often driven from their homes, can find themselves during their journey in deplorable, insupportable places. Unable to return to their lands of origin, they are forced to resettle in foreign lands where they frequently suffer from new traumas that are social, psychological, and economic. Often gender and generational differences cause turbulence within refugee families and cause new challenges to living together in foreign settings. This has been the case with some of the refugees of Romero House, and the community and the staff has had particular compassion for their situation during these traumatic events.

It is clear that dislocation causes significant suffering for people, especially women and children. In 1998, Canadian feminists set up a program called *Women at Risk* for refugee women faced with no local support, or who are not eligible under existing resettlement agreements. Even with this program, most women who are unskilled or who are caring for a number of children are passed over by Canada and other countries with similar programs.[17] A gathering of the women at Romero House often gives refugees a place to voice their concerns and receive some helpful suggestions, especially around issues concerning their children.

Theologically, the plight of the refugees raises the question of God, and spiritually it raises the question of response. Is God present in this global grief, and, if so, who is the God who permits this human suffering? What is the experience of those who minister with refugees, and how does an individual or community of faith respond to the forced flight of peoples in a world of unstable and dominant cultures? Although there are no easy answers to these questions, a contemplative theological reflection process such as the one entered into by the Romero House community offered one way to ponder these experiences and questions, and to decide how to engage the reality of the situation.

The Dominant Culture of North America

Canadian theologian Douglas Hall has characterized "the crisis of the dominant culture of North America as a particular species of the failure of the modern vision."[18] The vision of modernity emerged from humanistic thinkers of the Renaissance and slowly evolved through the Age of Enlightenment. Development escalated during the Industrial Revolution and intensified with the technological advances of the twentieth and now twenty-first centuries. As society has "advanced," there has been a gradual rejection of God and the Christian meaning of life. In the modern world the dominant Christian culture of the West has shifted its view from Jesus Christ as the revelation of the meaning of humanity in relation to God to a secular, materialistic, and scientific view of the world. Nietzsche's phrase "the death of God" captures the essence of this decline. Elie Wiesel's concept of "the death of man," born of his experience in the concentration camp, is an even more poignant phrase revealing the reality of the modern vision.

This vision was alive in the traditional Canadian government that took responsibility for the care of its citizens through many social contracts such as health care, education, public welfare, and job creation. The Angus Reid Group, a major Canadian research and polling service, states that most Canadians still believe that the main responsibility of the government is to "take care" of the people. However, in the late 1990s the *Toronto Star* announced that: "The cradle-to-grave welfare state is dead . . . the private sector is the mantra of a new and vigorous right." [19] This major ideological move is evident in the drastic cutbacks of the "Common Sense Revolution," which marks the end of the caring system that Canadians have always identified with the government. The refugees of the Romero House community have experienced the drastic result of these cutbacks, which took voice in the question: "How will I feed my children?"

Hall believes that this crisis can provide an opportunity for the Christian community to "contribute to the revolution of values and vision that global society requires of our continent." [20] He recognizes a potential for people of the Scriptures to face the disillusionment experienced at a time of failure or decline. To do this requires learning how to discern the "signs of the times" and courageously face the truth of our current critical realities. Since the events of 9/11, North America no longer trusts in a Utopian world, nor does it rely on the power of optimism. The challenge of all that opposes life is ever present. Hall hopes that with a renewed capacity for insightful judgment, people of goodwill might be able to examine the decline of the modern dream and explore its meaning and truth in order to begin again with renewed hope.[21]

During this time of "encircling gloom," Hall challenges the community of Christian disciples to contemplate and to assimilate from the Christian tradition the theology of the cross (*theologia crucis*). This requires a major shift from a culture oriented toward success to a public witness of the cross as "God's abiding commitment to the world." [22] In Hall's theology of the cross, God is experienced in "grace-given courage to engage the world." [23] Our group discerned this challenge, and the cross became a meaningful symbol for contemplative reflection as they prayed for the courage to remain faithful in their relationships with the refugees. They discerned a deeper call to solidarity as the image of these neighbors as the new crucified took shape.

THE POLITICAL "COMMON SENSE" REVOLUTION

The policy of recent past governments of Ontario, whose aim has been to balance the provincial budget, is haunted by the "Common Sense Revolution." This neoconservative approach to government values a profit-maximizing market, thereby protecting powerful central banks and limiting government action over international treaties and free trade. It reflects the economic policies initiated by the British Prime Minister Margaret Thatcher and adopted in the

United States by President Ronald Reagan. This neoconservative revolution culminated in 1992 in North America in the person of Newt Gingrich, Speaker of the House of Representatives of the United States from 1995–99. It became part of the fabric of the Ontario Harris government by 1994. To reduce the deficit in Ontario, for instance, the Conservative government under Premier Mike Harris instituted major cutbacks in the 1996 budget, one of which was a 21.6 percent reduction in welfare services.[24]

It cannot be denied that the debts of most governments need to be managed in a more responsible way. However, the drastic cuts to welfare recipients conveyed the message to the public not only that welfare recipients were the cause of the debt, but that the poor and disadvantaged were not a priority for the government. Many social justice groups have challenged this stance. It is now clear that government debt may also be linked to "tax breaks to the wealthy and corporations (50%) and high interest payments (44%), while only a small amount can be laid at the door of spending on social programs (2%)."[25] It is even questioned by some researchers whether or not there is a global trend to create large, low-wage labor forces in Ontario, similar to those in many less privileged countries.

It is obvious that the purpose in balancing the budget is complex, but the results of these cutbacks are real. In Toronto there has been a drastic increase in people needing shelters. Evictions of the poor are on the increase, and many of those on assistance are forced to pay rent rather than to buy food for their families. As a result most welfare recipients run out of money by the middle of the month. Research by "Toronto Action for Social Change" has discovered that, since the government cutbacks started, "the number of food banks in Canadian communities has increased 187%! In Metro Toronto, there are now more food banks than there are McDonalds."[26] The numbers of people needing access to these food banks, including refugees, is on the rise.

Every day across Canada, hungry people are served in food banks. "In March 2007 alone, 720,231 people were assisted by their local food bank. And the numbers have increased. Since 1997, food bank use has increased by 8.4%." Besides assistance with groceries the food banks served 2,344,462 meals in 2007.[27] These figures are representative of the consequences of governments continuing to value the "Common Sense Revolution."

Most refugees arrive in Canada without bringing any assets; for their first few months in the country they must subsist on welfare. In the meantime, the banks and corporations continue to profit from the interest on the government debt and taxes on the savings, goods, and services of the public. It is well known that despite the billions of dollars in profits, banks and corporations have contributed significantly less to the country's taxes over the last twenty-five years. This trend continues to be astonishingly relevant.

However, Canadians have increasingly become disillusioned by the government and are raising questions about the financial cutbacks. The polls have noted that the people want to eliminate wasteful spending but are critical of the government's failure in "not going after big corporations." "They are hitting single mothers and people on welfare." The National Affairs writer for the *Toronto Star* once described Canadians as "a people battered economically and bombarded ideologically; mistrustful of individual politicians but still looking to government; convinced of the need for public frugality but unwilling to let the state exit their lives entirely."[29]

With these descriptions in mind, I want to be conscious of the reality of my reflections in doing a theology of ministry in a context of the societal decline and instability of globalization. The economic, social, and cultural changes that refugees undergo as they battle within this environment present an enormous task for them and for their advocates. The effects of the cutbacks to welfare recipients were the major communal concern brought to this theological reflection process. It was both informative and inspiring to hear and read the reflections of the participants of this study. It raised my awareness once again of the importance of knowing the cultural context and economic struggle of those with whom we minister. It is becoming clearer to me that the structures of the government, banks, and corporations participating in a movement toward excessive profit are not "good news" but intensify a crucifixion of God's poor. On the other hand, the participants' struggle for prophetic faith and their witness of a compassion for their neighbors revealed the benefit of the Good News of the Gospel.

Chapter 5

REFLECTING FROM AND
WITH THE FAITH TRADITION

❖

The third step in the theological reflection process is to reflect theologically on insights of the faith tradition rising from the reinterpreted assumptions. This has the potential to lead one to see meaning in the experience. Theological traditions, issues, and the reality of the experience evoke the capacity to know the sacred in a lived experience.

REFLECTIONS ON FAITH TRADITION

For Christians, faith tradition is the belief that the presence of God is alive in the Spirit of Jesus Christ and in the life of the community. Christian tradition has the grace of transforming power in the lives of those who trust in God's love in Jesus Christ. Christians believe that God's mission is to assist the people of God in knowing what this love means in the life of the community. Struggling groups or individuals often return to the foundations of their faith for insight. Given the questions raised through a reflection by the Romero community, I have sought the wisdom of this living tradition, which supports the dynamics of conversion, a theology of the Cross, a vision of church, and an understanding of the ever-changing character of ministry.

Having been raised on a Vatican II theology in my adult years, I believed more in a theology of resurrection than in one of the Cross and tended to move through the passion to ponder the resurrection. In fact, we were encouraged to remember that we are an "Easter people." Imagine my surprise at the centrality the theology of the cross had in the final ritual surrounding the Romero House experience.

The questions of church and ministry arose not only in the Romero community and in my own reflections. There was a strong resistance in the group to the term *ministry*, for it conjured up clerical and professional images. Questions also arose about relationships with the institutional church, particularly for those on the edges of the structure of the church involved in compassionate ministry.

THE DYNAMICS OF CONVERSION

Hebrew Scripture Perspectives on Conversion

Shûb. The term most frequently used for conversion in the Hebrew Scriptures, *shûb* means a turning from faithlessness back to God. The Israelites were called to faithfulness in response to their founding religious experience, the covenant. Their personal relationship and covenant with God are at the heart of the meaning of *shûb*. "Yet even now, says the LORD, return to me with all your heart . . ." (Joel 2:12).

Shûb is used in reference to relationship in many instances in the Hebrew Scriptures. It refers to the collective conversion to God of the Hebrew People (The People of Sarah and Abraham), to conversion in the lives of individuals (e.g., David), and to the personal and social conversion in the vision of the prophets (e.g., Isaiah).

It is significant that both personal and communal conversions are part of the scriptural tradition. It is also important to note the place of social conversion in the context of the prophetic tradition. Societal conversion, particularly around the scriptural meaning of neighbor, was very meaningful to the participants in the reflection process at Romero House.

The prophet Isaiah, for example, realized that the people were unable to turn back to God because of their lack of *shûb*, or their hardness of heart. He looked to a remnant of people to be faithful to the divine covenant. Among a people that could not convert as a nation, the alternative became a community of disciples called to maintain fidelity to God and each other.

Later a new covenant and a new heart were promised to all nations through the prophet Jeremiah: "I will give them a heart to know that I am the LORD; and they shall be my people and I will be their God, for they shall return to me with their whole heart" (Jer 24:7).

> The old heart of the Sinai covenant had grown cold and thus unable to "know" the Lord, to live in intimate union with the Lord. The new heart promised by the Lord through Jeremiah held a deeper dimension of universalism. Now *all* (individuals and groups) will be able to "know" Yahweh through continual conversion and intimate love.[1]

A historical significance of this new and more inclusive covenant, with its call to ongoing conversion, was the impact it had on the evolution from the Hebrew story to the Christian story.

The meaning of *shûb*, as revealed in the stories of the Hebrew people, is consistent with many aspects of the stories revealed by the participants in this process of theological reflection. I am struck by the significance of a remnant group and an alternative model of community when societal conversion faces the social sin of a nation. The belief that God's power is stronger than social sin is evident in the reflections of the participants of Romero House.

Christian Scripture Perspectives on Conversion

From shûb *to* metánoia. While the Hebrew *shûb* connotes conversion in the Old Testament, the Greek *metánoia* is its counterpart in the Christian Scriptures. Conversion or turning to Jesus (*metánoia*) is the call demanded by the coming of the reign of God. For example, what is essentially distinct in the gospel story of the rich young man (Mark 10:17-31) is not the act of leaving all, which is not specifically

Christian, but being converted to Jesus. What is radical and new to the gospel is "the activity of following Jesus, which is qualified as an eschatological *metánoia*, an authentic conversion."[2]

In the New Testament there is also a shift in the context of conversion. The individual and the community of church, rather than the nation of Israel, are now the context of conversion.

> [M]ore stress is placed on individuals who are personally in-vited to conversion and who stand in need of continual conver-sion. On the other hand, the community composed of individuals—which was the house-based church—'the new Israel,' is seen needing continual conversion.[3]

The guiding vision for ongoing conversion also develops as we move from *shûb* to *metánoia*. The vision shifts from the covenant with God in the Hebrew Scriptures to the reign of God (*basileia*) in the Christian Scriptures.

Donald Gray includes "change of heart and reordering of priori-ties" in his translation of *metánoia*.[4] These are essential elements of repentance and are implied in the term *metánoia*; they give room for conversion in the life of Jesus.

Jesus' call to conversion. The prophetic call to repentance, con-tinual conversion, and intimate love evolved from the Hebrew Scrip-tures. In the Gospel of Mark, the first words of Jesus are a proclamation of the Good News and a call to conversion. "The time is fulfilled, and the reign of God has come near. Be converted and believe in the good news" (Mark 1:15, my translation). This echoes the Baptist and symbolizes Jesus' prophetic mission in the reign of God.

The baptism of Jesus and the reign of God (Basileia). Christian conversion is contingent on the experience of God's reign. The Gos-pel of Matthew speaks of "seeking" God, or the reign of God as the beginning of conversion. Jesus seeks this experience at his baptism. As part of the Jewish baptismal rite, there was an expression of yearning for the coming of the Messiah, the reign of God. At his baptism, "Jesus was not renouncing his sinfulness but was taking his place with all those in Israel who were saying: 'We are ready, Lord; please make this the moment of your Messianic salvation.'" [5]

It was in this process of seeking God that Matthew's Jesus responded to a call to conversion at his baptism.

> Jesus' experience at his baptism, so far as it can be recovered from the gospel records, seems in many respects akin to the psychological effects of a sudden conversion. There was a sudden and intense personal experience of God. There was a new awareness of personal status with God, a call to a new way of life and the acceptance of that call. There was, in fact, a reorientation of his whole personality. [6]

An experience of God can have a transforming effect in a person's life. While contemplating his baptism, Jesus experienced the Spirit of God assuring him: "You are my Son, the Beloved; with you I am well pleased" (Luke 3:22). Through this prayerful encounter, Jesus experienced a filial relationship with and an unconditional acceptance from God.

Grounded in this religious experience, Jesus reorganized his life and lived out *the* Christian parable for the sake of the reign of God. He changed priorities at the time of his baptism and moved from one way of living to another. "He gave up an earlier and long-standing way of life as no longer satisfactory in order to take up a new and perilous way of life that now seemed to him imperative." [7]

Through the conversion of his baptismal experience, Jesus turned to his mission and began his public ministry by proclaiming the reign of God. This is the context in which Jesus preached and lived his prophetic call to conversion. The reign of God is "the just and righteous purpose of God for all humanity." [8] After his baptism, Jesus continued the mission of announcing this vision of the *basileia* of God, which entails hearing, understanding, and doing the word of the *basileia* (Matt 13:23). Jesus enfleshes this vision of the reign of God in his compassionate encounters with those considered least, or the disadvantaged of society (Matt 25:40). [9]

Converted by the prophetic call of the reign of God, Jesus preached from this vision: "And now I will tell you what I will do to my vineyard" (Isa 5:5). He did not preach himself but proclaimed a confidence in the activity of God and responded by living in the presence of the reign of God.

> His most fundamental gesture is taking sides with human beings in a concrete situation where the existing political or religious structure has dehumanized people. . . . Jesus does all he can to concretize and make present real love as the quintessence of the kingdom.[10]

An example of a conversion in his public ministry occurs in the incident with the Canaanite woman and, therefore, an ethnic and religious outsider to Israel (Matt 15:21-28). She pleaded to Jesus for mercy for herself and healing for her daughter. Jesus understood his mission to be to the Israelite community and, at first, did not engage her in her petition. The disciples, lacking in understanding and compassion, wanted to send her away. Persistent, she continued to appeal to Jesus for help.

As Jesus listened to the woman, he was moved to enter into dialogue, and used a familiar parable about bread from the table not being thrown to dogs to oppose her request. Picking up the image of bread in this parable, the woman asked for crumbs from the master's table. Courageously, she claimed participation in the *basileia,* the reign of God, the dream of God for the community that Jesus was proclaiming. Jesus was moved by her faith, and through this dialogue he was converted to a more inclusive mission that embraced the Gentiles.

Jesus expressed inclusive love as he lived out his conversion to the vision of *basileia.* Jesus reveals his operative vision as he is seen eating with tax collectors and sinners (Matt 9:10-13), as he touches an unclean leper (8:3), as he is touched by a menstruating woman (9:20), as he has his vision of God's just purposes expanded by a Gentile woman (15:21-28), as he enters Jerusalem with a band of women and men from Galilee (21:1-11; 27:55), and as he gives his life for the sake of *basileia.*[11]

Jesus' vision of *basileia* is disclosed in the parables, revealing the compassion of God. The Prodigal Son, whose story typifies a universal human experience, is the central figure in one such parable.

The father, full of mercy, forgives the son when he declares his sin and unworthiness. Reconciliation and celebration are ritualized at the family homecoming party (Luke 15:11-32).

This parable speaks of mercy as the beginning of conversion. This is a significant indicator to the participants in this theological reflection process, as it exemplifies the movement from compassion to service in the lives of the participants at Romero House. God, the parent in the parable, delights in being merciful to us as loved children. God's love promises to help us change from hearts of stone to hearts of flesh; to lead us from self-absorption to responsible relationships; from angry reactions to compassionate service. A number of these conversions are noticeable in the meditations of participants as they reflect on their experience of compassion. Mercy, integral to compassion, is the source and summons of the process of conversion.[12]

Jon Sobrino echoes the role of God's mercy in the life of Jesus as he responded to his baptismal conversion in acts of justice. In *The Principle of Mercy*, Sobrino calls the loving activity of God and the gestures of Jesus *mercy*. God, who saw the suffering, heard the cry, and knew the pain of the Israelites, was moved to liberate them (Exod 3:7-8). The penetration of the heart on behalf of the suffering of others Sobrino calls the *principle of mercy*.[13]

Jesus' vision of God is of one who defends the suffering and is merciful to the poor. His praxis was on behalf of the vulnerable, and Jesus is often portrayed in the gospels as challenging the laws of the time and risking his life for this vision of mercy. The parable of the man with the withered hand exemplifies this (Mark 3:1-6). Jesus considered it a priority to heal the person despite the law of the Sabbath that forbids this. His merciful action led to his condemnation. "The Pharisees went out and immediately conspired with the Herodians against him, how to destroy him" (Mark 3:6).

Compassion became a meaningful metaphor for the participants of this study. Reflection on the suffering of the refugees, whom they saw as the contemporary crucified, was balanced by their hope in the power of their discipleship in Jesus, often giving the participants the courage to face the risks present in their daily lives of service.

The gospel events of the baptism of Jesus, his public ministry and indeed his life, death, and resurrection, are the Christian parables par excellence that challenge the community of faith to live a life of ongoing conversion.

Like Job, the conversion of a just person moves the person not from evil to good but from a life of goodness to a radical surrender of the self to God. The life of Jesus reveals this conversion as he moves from baptism to ministry and into his death. In his ministry he encounters failure, and eventually his journey leads to the cross. As Sallie McFague says, "the cross—an obviously 'worldly' rejection—is itself the *great parable*, the inversion of all inversions, the subverter of all worldly standards and comforts, for here life is gained only through death."[14]

At death, Jesus struggled and yielded in dependence on the power of God. In his resurrection he was liberated. He left his disciples, inviting them to be at one with him in the liberation of his resurrection. For his disciples or followers, this implies a call to ongoing conversion and a summons to continue the prophetic call of compassionate living.

The mystery of this story of Jesus' conversion was an inspiration to the theological reflection group. They gained insight and the courage to follow in discipleship as they reflected on the life of Jesus and their life with the refugees.

Contemporary Theological Insights on Conversion

Most contemporary theologians agree with classical Christian wisdom that God initiates the process of conversion. In describing this initiative, Bernard Lonergan uses the scriptural image of God's love flooding our hearts through the Holy Spirit given us in Christ (Rom 5:5).[15]

Both Elizabeth Johnson and Karl Barth use the image of "awakening" to describe how one becomes aware of the realities of God. The metaphor of awakening places the individual in a movement that reveals the truth that God is "for them" and they are "for God." This movement of the twofold "for" makes for a life of ongoing conversion with the second "for" grounded in the first "for."[16]

However, we have also been given the freedom to refuse, to resist, this invitation. Any movement toward responding to the possibility of conversion is already the movement of God's grace within us. As I listened to the participants in this theological reflection process, I heard them say frequently that they were changed through events that were not of their making, through persons and situations that were beyond their control. Conversion is a gift of grace.

Conversion and Relational Grace

Joanne Wolski Conn defines grace as "God's offer of loving relationship and a sharing in God's own life, which is freely given and initiates this relationship." [17] From this perspective, grace is a participating relationship with God that respects the divinity of God and the boundaries of the self. God is known and experienced as One who is at home with us and yet never fully comprehended. The self is called in freedom and autonomy into mutual relationship with God, present in community and revealed in Jesus. In other words, it is through relationship that God is known as God and the human being as a human being. A relational image of God frequently appeared in the meditations of the participants in this theological reflection process.

An individual is both free to make autonomous decisions and capable of entering into shared relationships. Such relational decisions are important to the process of conversion. As I engaged in this process, it became evident that the relationships the volunteers had with each other and with the refugees influenced their relationship with God, and their relationship with God changed their relationship to each other and to the refugees.

Elizabeth Johnson also articulates conversion in relational terms and is helpful in understanding some of the developments within the service of compassionate ministry. According to her, conversion is the awakening of gifts of the Spirit, which challenges relationships to be mutual and courageous. Awakening is the empowerment of the Spirit. It releases the capabilities of giftedness in both the individual and in the communal experience of conversion. Conversion is

a permanent process of both turning away and turning toward—turning away from all that intellectually, morally and
spiritually keeps one mired in abusive relationships characterized by domination, intimidation, fear, or dishonesty and turning toward the unlimited grace of God ever calling us to
relationships characterized by mutuality, respect, courage and
truthfulness.[18]

Conversion empowers and affirms one's strength and responsibility.
It is the movement toward the appropriation of the relational gifts
within an individual, group, or society.

Sin in a Relational Context

If grace and conversion are understood in relational terms, how
then can we understand sin? A relational view of sin is the refusal
to enter into relationship. It is the choice to remain an isolated, autonomous individual.[19] This view sees the modern choice for autonomy as a "sinful" form of individualism.

However, contemporary feminists have quite rightly pointed
out that such an understanding of sin can work against the important
and positive process of individuation. They are wary of the oblitera-
tion of the self that can take place in a group. This view of sin must
take account the necessary process of individuation without fostering individualism. In some of the documents of Vatican II, an attempt was made to balance these two concerns.[20]

It is helpful to note that contemporary thinker John Macmurray
makes a distinction between the *individual* who finds freedom in
autonomy and the *person* who finds freedom and identity only
through relationship. He realizes that the "capacity for communion,
that capacity for entering into free and equal personal relations, is
the thing that makes us human."[21] In this more "personalist" approach, persons find their true selves and true identity only in and
through relationship. The refusal of relationship is, then, also a refusal to become one's true self.

This notion of sin and grace in relational terms can be expanded
beyond the immediately personal to the wider social context. When

we are unable or unwilling to see our lives in relationship to all other human beings, then we are more likely to become unjust, violent, and hate filled.

This notion of sin and grace seemed evident in the material that emerged from the theological reflection with the Romero staff. It seemed obvious that those who had a close personal relationship with the refugees became personally involved and sought justice for them as persons; those whose relationships with the refugees were more distant looked on them more as problem cases to be solved by examining the issues concerning their particular situations.

DIMENSIONS OF CONVERSION

Bernard Lonergan describes Christian conversion as God flooding our hearts through the Holy Spirit given in Christ.[22] Conversion, through the work of the Spirit, enables persons to make new judgments and decisions and to move beyond established concerns or horizons into new horizons of knowing, valuing, and acting. Conversion takes place on many levels in the lives of individuals; it has a transforming effect on all of one's relationships. As Lonergan notes:

> It is not merely a change or even a development; rather, it is a radical transformation on which follows, on all levels of living, an interlocked series of changes and developments. What hitherto was unnoticed becomes vivid and present. What had been of no concern is a matter of high import. So great a change in one's apprehensions and one's values accompanies no less a change in oneself, in one's relations to other persons, and in one's relations to God.[23]

> Conversion can be dramatic or slow, intimate but not solitary, concrete and communal, dynamic and ongoing.[24]

And so it is for the participants in this process.

Reflection on conversion is fundamental to religious living and relationship. Lonergan specifies that "reflection on the *ongoing process of conversion* may bring to light the real foundation of renewed theology."[25] Such reflection, especially on individual and communal relationships, was at the foundation of the process with the Romero staff.

Dean Brackley sheds light on Lonergan's understanding of the search for truth as ongoing conversion of the whole person. He reframes Lonergan's search for truth as knowing the "heart of reality" that places one at the door of the mercy of God. Such knowing requires the practice of four interconnected imperatives: first, be attentive to reality; second, be intelligent, that is, think this reality through; third, be reasonable, that is, seek genuine insights that correspond to this reality; and finally, be responsible, that is, discern and decide the action that love requires. These imperatives will lead one to authenticity and Mystery.

Brackley also offers a challenge to the work of Lonergan by suggesting the provocative question: Be attentive to *what*; that is, to *whose reality* do we attend? From his experience of ministry among the victims of society, Brackley encourages us to be attentive to the reality of the poor, whom the Gospel tells us will lead to the heart of reality, the Mystery of God. As the participants of this theological reflection process were attentive to the realities of the refugees, they were led to authentic compassion and the heart of Mercy.[26]

In an inspiring comment, Lonergan expresses the value of the communal aspect of theological reflection when he says that conversion

> can happen to many and they can form a community to sustain
> one another in their self-transformation, and help one another
> in working out the implications, and in fulfilling the promise
> of their new life. Finally, what can become communal can
> become historical. It can pass from generation to generation.
> It can spread from one cultural milieu to another. It can adapt
> to changing new situations, survive into a different age, and
> flourish in another period or epoch.[27]

The influence that one generation had on another in the group dynamic I observed gives credence to the historical aspect of conversion. The hope engendered in the participants' reflections and their experience of conversion promises new life for each of them and for those in relationship with them. I noted a transforming effect in the hope and service they bring to the Romero House community. The group's influence on the refugee advocacy community in Toronto is also apparent in the informed networking and the mutual encouragement that has emerged within these groups.

Relying on Lonergan, Donald Gelpi names five human tendencies that, given a graced reality, can aid five kinds of conversion. Self-reflection, of course, enables developmental change in each dimension.

(1) Affective conversion promotes healthy personal emotional development.

(2) Intellectual conversion promotes true beliefs about reality, whether one reaches those beliefs intuitively or rationally.

(3) Personal moral conversion ensures responsible interpersonal relationships.

(4) Sociopolitical conversion promotes the ongoing reform of unjust social structures.

(5) Religious conversion responds to the divine touch on the terms set by God. [28]

Each of these dimensions of conversion was represented in the variety of reflections by the staff and volunteers of the Romero community. Every participant experienced some personal and social change in each of the five kinds of conversion.

Ultimately, the change in the individuals and the community had something to do with the change in their relationship to Jesus as they reflected on his life in the gospels. Through companionship with Jesus and with others, they were converted on all levels of being and this conversion led to fuller companionship. The fruit of conversion, as a transformation of conscience, is loving compassion. Walter Conn's thinking on the pattern of conversion in the life of Thomas Merton is helpful in this regard. Christian conversion reorients a person's whole life to truth, value, love, and the experience of God as it is shaped by the Christian story.

> The personal measure of Christian living, therefore, is the conscience which has experienced a Christian conversion at once

cognitive, affective, moral, and religious. Only a person thus converted is fully and concretely sensitive to the loving life of Jesus. In Merton's life we discovered again the fundamental Gospel truth that lies at the heart of Christian tradition: the radical religious conversion of Christian conscience finds its fullest realization in loving compassion—the self-transcending perfection of human empathy and justice.[29]

Conn demonstrates through the life of Merton that the true self and God are both discovered in contemplation, which liberates the conscience for conversion. Through contemplation, self-transcending love and compassion are found to be at the heart of the converted Christian.

The fruit of such conversion is evident in the reflection on the life of Jesus and in the compassion it engendered in the hearts of the participants. It was clear that both the autonomy of the individual and a willingness to surrender to the needs of the refugees were part of the struggle. The mystery of Christ was seen especially through contemplation on the suffering of the refugees and reflection on the cross and resurrection of Christ. Each was an inspiring reality in this reflection process.

The noteworthy German theologian Karl Rahner writes about conversion as a grace and a decision made not once but daily. He understands that "to commit the whole of life to God" is the fundamental choice of the human being.[30] Conversion as a free and reflective decision about a fundamental relation to God reflects the biblical perspective of response to the initial call of God. Freedom to turn to God is only possible through the gift of grace, a "participation in the divine life itself." Conversion involves a personal call from God for the sake of the reign of God. For the Christian, this is a call to participate in the presence of God in the person of Jesus Christ.

Rahner understands this call as the summons to receive the gift of God's self-communication. With this utterance from God, a response is possible and liberates one from the idols of self and sin. More positively, Rahner considers the response of conversion evident in the following experiences of grace: detachment from self, love of neighbor, trusting the meaningfulness of life without determining control over it, and accepting God as the ultimate source of life. The radical character of Christian conversion imposes serious obligations, because faith in Jesus, crucified and risen, involves the call of God. For Rahner, this self-disclosure of God, present in the life, death, and resurrection of Jesus, makes conversion possible for the Christian.

Rahner believes that conversion is a gift of God's grace and a decision concerning the whole of one's life. Conversion includes the theological virtues of faith, hope, and charity. It is faith in the call of God and reception of the call. It is hope in the capacity to trust the unknown and be available for God. It is charity in the freedom to trust in history and in the particular love of neighbor in whom "one knows with genuine personal knowledge who God is."

Rahner notes the importance of each moment of conversion by insisting that conversion requires daily fidelity. "It is a sobering realization that every conversion is only a beginning and that the rest of daily fidelity, the conversion which can only be carried out in a whole lifetime, has still to come."[31] Conversion, then, is ongoing and requires daily fidelity to the fundamental decision to commit the whole of one's life to God, through love of neighbor in whom one knows a personal experience of God.

Rahner's theology of conversion is of particular interest to me because some of the conditions he stipulates are found in the participants in this process of theological reflection. Hope is in the unknown, love of neighbor, and faith in God.

THEOLOGY OF THE CROSS

The cross of Christ can never be separated from the prophets of Israel and from what Abraham Heschel calls "the pathos of God." Heschel believes that "God is concerned about the world and shares its fate. Indeed, this is the essence of God's moral nature: His willingness to be intimately involved in history."[32] Divine pathos is God's commitment to the suffering of creation. It is the compassion of God, God's mercy, God's *hesed* (Exod 20:6; Isa 54:8; Ps 136).

In the Christian Scriptures, the commitment of God to love and liberate all of creation is the foundation of the theology of the cross. "For God so loved the world that he gave his only Son, so that everyone who believes in him may not perish but may have eternal life" (John 3:16). Dietrich Bonhoeffer referred to the prophetic tradition of redemption when he wrote of the cross in his last letters before his execution or martyrdom. For Bonhoeffer,

> the difference between the Christian type of resurrection and theological hope is that the former sends a man back to his life on earth in a wholly new way, which is even more sharply defined than it is in the Old Testament. The Christian . . . like Christ himself must drink the earthly cup to the dregs, and only in doing so is the crucified and risen Lord with him, and he crucified and risen with Christ.[33]

Bonhoeffer's words continue to be prophetic today. His witness is a challenge to communities committed to the theology of the cross and moved, through the revelation of God's compassion, to the suffering of others.

The crucifixion was a result of the activity and ministry of Jesus. The cross stands for his compassionate service and is the antithesis of dominating power. The inclusive circle of disciples who gathered around Jesus and his prophetic words and deeds of healing were too much for the political and religious powers (Luke 9:22) of the day. His radical life, as he set his face toward Jerusalem, was more the signature of his death than a requirement of God for sin (Luke 9:51).

The cross is a parable of God's participation in the suffering of the world. Jesus' death was an act of violence brought about by threatened human men, an act of sin and therefore against the will of a gracious God. It occurred historically in consequence of Jesus' fidelity to the deepest truth and love he knew, expressed in his message and behavior. . . . The gracious God of Jesus enters into solidarity with all those who suffer.[34]

The ministry and death of Jesus manifests his option for the poor, suffering, and excluded of his world. The cross reveals the compassion and mercy of God directed toward liberating the oppressed and establishing right relationships for all creation.

It is my sincere belief that the participants in this reflection were engaged in a form of political theology and ethics when they chose the cross of the Christ as an icon for their political, prayerful vigil. The cross gave them a way of identifying pain and political suffering but also of lifting this up into a whole theological context of meaning. With this in mind, I want to consider living out this theology, through discipleship, in the community of the church.

ECCLESIOLOGY AND MINISTRY

It is believed by the post–Vatican II Christian community that the mission of the church is to further the reign of God. The mission of the church is to continue the healing and humanizing of God, revealed most explicitly in the person of Jesus, the Christ.

The importance of a recovered sense of history is significant because, very simply, all reality, especially human reality, exists in time. The very core of our Christian faith is built on a historical fact—Jesus of Nazareth, a human person who lived in our world, who is alive and who relates to us in the present moment. Because he was then and there, he can be here and now. And this is our hope—that Jesus is and will be everywhere.[35]

With this sense of Christian history, and centered in the hope of the continual presence of the Christ, I consider the history of ministry in the life of the church, beginning with the historical Jesus. From my experience with the Romero community, I wonder if ministry is a meaningful metaphor for baptized Christians in a postmodern society and a post–Vatican II church.

The ministry of Jesus was informed through his experience and image of God. The *Abba* experience, his filial relationship with God (Mark 14:36), enabled him to engage in his mission and proclaim the reign of God (Luke 4:43). Elizabeth Johnson suggests that he ministered as a "prophet" of the God of Wisdom. As Wisdom, Jesus was "Sophia sent to announce that God is the God of all-inclusive love who wills the wholeness and humanity of everyone, especially the poor and heavily burdened."[36] This wisdom, flowing from his relationship with Sophia, enabled him to engage in words and deeds of compassion and liberation.

Through his practice of ministry at an inclusive community table, Jesus "widened the circle of the friends of God" to include the most devalued persons. In his ministry Jesus preached hope and empowered acts of compassion in the liberating relationships he had with both women and men.[37]

The gospel that Jesus preached had the reign of God (*basileia*) as its context. Through parables, Jesus revealed such truths as what the *basileia* is like, relationships that reveal the reign of God and how this vision can transform human structures and action. The miracles of Jesus are concrete actions that provide healing to the sick and liberation for the oppressed. Jesus is joined along the way by a "circle of twelve disciples," which evolves into a movement or a community of followers.[38] This circle image reminds me of the circle around the Romero House table and the community circling Queen's Park for the ritual.

The enlarged circle of Jesus' disciples is his "community of life." This community included "men and women, the marginalized and the religiously observant, tax collectors and sinners. . . . Life together, made it possible to experience in the praxis of the *basileia* the proclaimed message of the inbreaking reign of God."[39]

This community of life or *ekklesia* reflects what Elisabeth Schüssler Fiorenza calls a "discipleship of equals" that can bring about the *basileia*. Community makes present the "life-giving power" of God in the midst of the "death-dealing powers" of oppression and dehumanization, to establish "an alternative world of justice and well being." Jesus created community by inviting people to gather around the table in justice and love, and from there went forth to feed the hungry, heal the sick, and liberate the oppressed.[40] This movement from table to service mirrors the dynamic of the Romero House community and the small reflective group who participated in the critical process of theological reflection.

The early ministers of the gospel eventually moved from Jesus' pattern of preaching and healing to proclaiming Jesus as the content of the gospel. "The content of the gospel is now that Jesus is the Christ" continuing his healing and humanizing mission.[41]

Through the community of the church, ministry is intended to serve the vision of God that in grace sets forth acts of justice and mercy. What model of church would foster such a vision? What theology of ministry would animate the message of this loving mission of God?

One possible answer in light of this reflection process is the model of communal discipleship. This best represents the image of church reflective of the ministry of the Romero community.

No single model of church reflects the mystery of the presence of God and our humble efforts at appropriating this presence. Avery Dulles originally used five models of church (institution, sacrament, communion, herald, and servant) as a framework for ecclesiology. He later expanded his work by developing a discipleship and ecclesial community as a paradigm for church.[42] The community of disciples harmonizes these five models of church and contributes a contemporary ecclesiology for a theology of ministry.

According to Johannes Metz, discipleship is a radical Christian stance that involves keeping alive the "dangerous memory" of Jesus Christ. Forms of religious commitment to this objective have emerged throughout the history of the church. Some of the participants of this study boldly aspire to a radical lay commitment they refer to as a "new monasticism." As a small faith community in service of "the other," they rely on the dangerous memory of Jesus, the Christ.

It is clear from Scripture and tradition that Christian spirituality calls all baptized to bring the Gospel to the contemporary world. This model is found in many basic Christian and covenant communities. I would include the Romero House community among them.

The documents of Vatican II, particularly *Lumen Gentium*, emphasize that the church does not have a mission but rather participates in God's mission (*missio Dei*) to the world. Through these documents the church is called to know itself not as the medium of God's action but as a sign or instrument of this action happening through all parts of the world.

Guiding the participants in this reflection was clearly a ministry experience for me. However, as mentioned earlier, some members of the group were unwilling to accept the term "ministry" for their accompaniment of the refugees and their support of the homeless they met along the way. They felt the term to be professional, and we did not take time for an in-depth study around the relationship of ministry and baptism.

Throughout the history of the church, the concept of grace (*charisma*) of baptism dispersed among the many members of the community has shifted to the notion that ministry is confined to a specialized charisma of a few. By the first half of the third century, ministry began to be institutionalized canonically and liturgically. The distinctive rites of ordination, which became part of the tradition for designating bishops, presbyters, and deacons, are in the writings of Hippolytus (d. 235). A local church had authority to "set apart" a member for a "share in spiritual service" of the whole community. This is the origin of the word "clergy," which was first used by Origen in the third century to denote the ministers of the church, in contrast to the laity. The distinction was used in this narrow sense by Jerome and led to the division of clergy and laity when Christianity became the state religion in the fourth century.[43] I believe this distinction contributes to the reason why members of the church do not recognize their baptismal grace of service as ministry.

Despite these complexities, history has taught us that the Spirit of the Resurrected Christ continues to be available for the conversion of the church and the transformation of the world. Ministry is defined by Thomas O'Meara in the following way: "Christian ministry is the public activity of a baptized follower of Jesus Christ flowing from the Spirit's charism and an individual personality on behalf of a Christian community to witness to, serve and realize the kingdom of God."[44] I believe that the members of the reflection group of Romero House are participating in this transformation and definition of ministry. However, the word ministry had "professional" overtones for many in the group, and they had difficulty identifying with the term. It is interesting to note that they felt the same toward "professional" social workers, lawyers, and other service personnel. In light of this tension, the participants understood themselves more as "disciples of Jesus," responding in "compassionate service" while trying to "do justice" in society. Through their eyes, I can now see a spirituality of ministry as a way in which a community of disciples can engage in prophetic service.

THE PROPHETIC DIMENSION OF DOING THEOLOGY

David Tracy's work explores the prophetic dimension of theology. He introduces the image of God as the Other, revealed in those who disclose the Sacred. "Christian theology at its best is the voice of the Other through all those others who have tasted, prophetically and meditatively, the Infinity disclosed in the kenotic reality of Jesus Christ."[45]

A prophetic and contemplative disposition helps a Christian theologian discern the voice of the Other, the voice of God, in the other. This prayerful practice reveals a prophetic image of God as being foundational to doing theology.

Tracy describes the revelation of the Other as the gift or grace from an event that disrupts the sameness of life. This disruption comes when we pay attention to the other, or "turn to the other." The "prophetic" phrase is from the postmodern philosopher Emmanuel Levinas, who claims that the face of postmodernity is the face of the threatened other commanding, "Do not kill me."

In this postmodern world, God is revealed in events of the other and their otherness. This harkens back to Bracken's imperative of attending to the reality of the poor. In ministry, as we pay attention, we recognize that the Other is present in the one who is different, or of no account to the dominant culture. The suffering and oppression of today requires ethical and mystical reflection by contemporary theologians.

God's shattering otherness, the neighbor's irreducible otherness, the "othering" reality of "revelation," . . . all these expressions come in new, postmodern and post-neoorthodox forms to demand the serious attention of all thoughtful theologians.[46]

Tracy's advice that we give serious attention to the other was realized in my experience of reflection with the Romero community. This attention to the other was apparent in their written reflections and in their conversations, though they did not consider themselves theologians or ministers, but "disciples of Christ." They saw the presence of God in the otherness of the poor and in the refugees they encountered. The Romero community preferred to relate to the others, the refugees, not as foreigners but as neighbors.

For Tracy, to be a thoughtful and ethical Christian theologian and minister today, one must recover the mystical readings of the prophetic and meditative (wisdom) traditions of the Bible. From these two religious forms and their dialectic, there will emerge a "fuller spectrum of past, present and likely future forms of Christian theology."

The prophetic stories of the Bible, and meditating on the mystical realities of the life of Christ were important sources of reflection for the Romero community. Again, they did not use theological language but spoke of the "prophets of old" and the "mystery" of the life of "Jesus, a prophet" who "surrendered his life for love of others." The mystery of the cross and resurrection were central to their vision of "hope" in and for the "others," and for their own "prophetic courage" to continue their Christian commitments.

Doing theology is a process of searching for the revelation of the living God in the midst of life. It is my deep belief that the God of compassion was revealed to a small community of faith and service through a process of theological reflection. This living presence of God arose from the stories of suffering, experiences of service, and questions of faith of the Romero House community. This reflective experience on compassionate service enabled each of us to participate in a transforming process of ongoing conversion. During this reflection, participants experienced a revitalized image of God's compassion.

A RENEWED IMAGE OF MINISTRY

This theological reflection manifested a renewed image of ministry to me. The image of the circle is now pierced with a cross and transformed into a Celtic cross (✟). This ancient and familiar image now has a deeper meaning for me. The circle represents the womb-love of God (*rahamim*) and the compassionate care of the disciple-ship of equals. The form of the circle is now scored through by the beams of the cross to represent the suffering of others as it reveals the mystery of the Other. The horizon of the circle is expanded and converted by the extension of the cross, stretched by the renewed values of the theology of the cross and a creative meaning of God's mercy and compassion. I believe the suffering others in this post-modern era can be strengthened and healed through communities contemplating the mystery of the cross of Christ and reaching out in compassion. Christian ministry includes participating in a community of equal discipleship, contemplating the prophetic dimension of a theology of the cross and collaborating in compassionate care for the reality and revelation of the Other.

Chapter 6

INTEGRATING SPIRITUALITY
INTO THE REFLECTION PROCESS

❖

The fourth step in this process of theological reflection calls for a reflection on the spirituality of an experience and a conscious decision for transformed action. Spirituality, the lived expression of faith, is relational if one believes in a personal God. The new action may range from a decision to reflect more on the experience, to a response of compassion to the suffering of another, to a change in attitude. All the physical, spiritual, rational, intuitive, and relational capabilities are involved in a decision to respond from a contemplative stance.

REFLECTING ON SPIRITUALITY

Spirituality is the religious and human experience of living from an internalized vision of faith. Spirituality flows from our relationship with the God of our faith tradition. For Christians, God is revealed in the life, death, and resurrection of Jesus Christ and in the power of the Spirit gifted to the believing community. Spirituality has three interpretations in the current culture. First, it is the human capacity to move beyond self-interest and to reach out to others in love, freedom, and truth. This potential for "self-transcendence is the core of any definition of spirituality." [1] Second, spirituality reflects the religious dimension of life, as self-transcendence is set free by what one believes to be the Holy. Third, spirituality refers to the religious experience of certain groups, such as Jewish, Christian, Muslim, or Buddhist. To my mind, this particular experience of ministry includes all three understandings of spirituality, particularized through the personalities and graced experience of the Romero House community. My reflection on their compassionate response in faith to self-transcendence caused me to seek deeper understanding of the role of compassion in ministry.

The spirituality of compassion. The metaphor of compassion is an image present in the ministry of Jesus, the community of disciples, and in the reflections of the group. Christian spirituality identifies compassion with tenderness, pity, and mercy.

The word "mercy," as it is used in the biblical tradition, represents my experience of the stories of compassion revealed in this study. In the Hebrew Scriptures a word that brings life and heart to the notion of "mercy" is *rahamim*, the empathetic "womb-love" of Yhwh, a word rich in meaning.

Rahamim implies a physical response; the compassion for another is felt in the center of one's body; it is an upsurge of mercy that also results in action. It is a word frequently predicated of Yhwh who has deep mother-love (Isa 49:15; Jer 31:20) or strong father-love (Ps 103:13; Isa 63:15-16) for Israel.[2]

Mercy, or compassion, is the capacity to be moved, through a depth of feeling, by the vulnerability of another. The God of Rachel expressed this in giving hope for her future and a promise that her children would come home (Jer 31:15-17). The God of Ephraim expressed this with the words: ". . . I am deeply moved . . . I will surely have mercy . . ." (Jer 31:20). Mercy requires the sensitivity and risk to alleviate tragedy imaged in a parent's love for a child. Mercy is tenderness moved into action for the other.

For Christians, the compassion of God is known through the life of Jesus, the Christ. ". . . I desire mercy and not sacrifice . . ." (Matt 12:7) is exemplified in Jesus' preaching and healing (Matt 9:36; 14:14; 25:31-46), in his care for suffering humanity (Luke 19:41), and in his self-sacrificial love on the cross (Rom 5:8). Jesus provided parables of compassion for his circle of friends, in such stories as the father "moved with mercy" (Luke 15:20, my translation), and the good Samaritan.

In the parable of the Good Samaritan, the figure of the robber represents an "infantile position: what is yours is mine." The priest on the other hand, represents the "narcissistic worldview: what is mine is mine." The Samaritan, moved to compassion for a neighbor, demonstrates the "altruistic posture: what is mine is yours."[3] (Similar insights were mentioned in the reflections of the participants at Romero House.)

In this parable the Samaritan went about his business while at the same time caring for the needs of another. He did not neglect his journey, as he relied on others in the community to support his service. The Samaritan represents a developmentally mature minister "having compassion" for another. The "good minister" is depicted by Jesus as capable of harmonizing love of self, the other, and God, as he cares for the other, trusts the innkeeper, and moves on about his concerns. Authentic self-sacrifice values both mutuality and interdependence. Jesus upholds these values. He teaches in this parable about God's compassion and the neighbor's service to the suffering stranger.[4]

The parable of the Good Samaritan is an important parable in light of the challenge to respond to the needs of the suffering of others. It offers a valuable vision of a community of care working together. Romero House community, as it provides for the needs of its members, is an example of compassionate service. This parable reveals a model of the "good minister," discerning how to balance compassionate relationships while being about the journey of life.

Jon Sobrino emphasizes the scriptural meaning of mercy by insisting that the quality of mercy be a principle for action on behalf of the suffering peoples. He asserts that not only individuals suffer in this world, but that whole groups of peoples are crucified. For Sobrino, the principle of mercy is the enfleshment of a compassionate response to remove crucified people from the cross. When I think of the refugees from Latin America, Africa, the Middle East, and other troubled lands served by Romero House, I believe I witness Sobrino's principle of mercy becoming action for justice.[5]

Maria Clara Bingemer states that the mission of Jesus, in his life of compassionate service, revealed *rahamim*, God's merciful love for the world. As a mother's womb contains the pain and suffering, the hurts and sorrow of the oppressed, those involved in compassionate ministry are called to bear witness through felt love and action on behalf of the wounded of the world. A compassionate response to suffering is tough but tender, firm but without violence, engaged in the struggle but able to celebrate life and faith.[6]

I have witnessed a care in the Romero community that is firm, tender, and celebrative. For this reason, I consider them to be engaged in compassionate ministry. By facilitating this ministry, I also am summoned to compassion and conversion of heart and action.

THE PROCESS OF ONGOING CONVERSION

Before engaging in this theological reflection project, I assumed that the participants of this theological reflection process would be in a process of "ongoing conversion," not turning from a life of sin to a life with God. They confirmed this at our first meeting when they affirmed that they hoped for a "deeper relationship with God," and desired to serve with a "gospel vision."

Christian conversion, then, is an ongoing process. It begins with a state of awareness of God's call to live differently to the final integration of conversion nurtured within the context of the Christian community. It includes all the events of resistance and revelation as well as the in-between decisions. These decisions, primarily about relationships, need to be encircled in a reflective quality of living.

Ongoing Christian conversion is the turning around of heart and mind in response to the Gospel of Christ. It encompasses compassionate responses made in the interpersonal encounter of the face of Christ in experience, culture, creation, and the historical religious tradition.

CONVERSION:
THE WEAVE OF CONTEMPLATION AND ACTION

Conversion is not only a call or an invitation, but it is also the grace to respond to what is contained within that call. How that call and one's response take place can be influenced by different internal psychological dynamics. It may also be influenced by the person's particular historical-social context. Persons may enter into a process of conversion through contemplation, or they may do so through engaging in a particular action.

Thomas Merton is a contemporary example of someone whose conversion from isolation and separateness into relationship with God and with all of humanity took place primarily through a deepening process of contemplation.

Merton makes a distinction between the false self, which is under the illusion that it is the whole self, and the true self, which is dependent on God.[7] For Merton, the true self is known to be naturally self-transcending and capable of a deep relationship with God who is alive in the heart of the true self. This truth is awakened through contemplation, an experience in which we humbly realize that God dwells in the mystery of our true self. It is because God is related to us that we become our true selves. It is when we see that we are radically related through God to all other human beings that we risk choices that demand justice and compassion for the needs and rights of others. In *New Seeds for Contemplation*, Merton notes:

> Every expression of the will of God is in some sense a "word" of God. By this I do not mean continuous "talk," or a frivolous form of affective prayer. . . . but a dialogue of love and of choice. A dialogue of deep wills. . . .
>
> Whatever is demanded by truth, by justice, by mercy, or by love must surely be willed by God.[8]

This conviction was surely influenced by an earlier experience in Merton's life as a monk. While walking across the street at the corner of Fourth and Walnut, in Louisville, Kentucky, Merton had

a revelation about the importance of being connected and loving in
the world, even in a world of strangers:

> I was suddenly overwhelmed with the realization that I loved
> all those people, that they were mine and I theirs, that we could
> not be alien to one another even though we were total strang-
> ers. It was like waking up from a dream of separateness, of
> spurious self-isolation in a special world, the world of renun-
> ciation and supposed holiness. The whole illusion of a separate
> holy existence is a dream.[9]

For Merton, sin is the refusal to accept the self as capable of self-
transcendence, as dependent on God, yet free to make decisions for
the sake of relationship.

For Merton, the value of contemplation as a method of discover-
ing and integrating the true self moves this process into a religious
reality. For the participants at Romero House, contemplation as part
of the theological reflection process was also of inestimable value in
contributing to the participants' self-knowledge and freedom.

It is also possible for some people to be converted as they are
placed or as they place themselves within a new context, a new reality. Richard Rohr writes about conversion through contemplation
and action—living the realities of life:

> What converts people are circumstances, real life situations.
> What changes people are confrontations, looking at something
> they don't want to deal with straight in the face, or looking at
> life from a new vantage point. . . . Reality is the greatest ally
> of God. What *is* converts us. That is full incarnation.[10]

The participants of Romero House can attest to this, for they entered
what was truly the world of "the other," the outcast and the
marginalized.

It is my conviction that action, when accompanied by subsequent reflection and ongoing contemplation, is a locus for conversion. Engagement in a ministry of compassionate service, which is
the fruit of conversion, is also the seed of ongoing conversion.

The Beginning of Conversion

It seems obvious that the Romero House participants were in a process of conversion when they began the theological reflection project and, indeed, indicated this by making the decision to come to Romero House. There is the mystery of grace in the call to conversion and in the decision to respond. It is a process, as Rahner says, that involves the whole of one's life.[11]

Because the participants were in a process of conversion, they came to a decision to change their lives—where they lived, how they lived, and what they would do. They entered a place where they would be involved in the works of mercy—feeding the hungry, clothing the cold, visiting those who have been imprisoned and tortured. They changed the reality of their lives—and that probably made all the difference to their changing perspective on life.

Richard Rohr has written that while people may be inspired by talks from teachers such as himself, they are seldom changed by them. What changes people, he says, is experiencing reality. People are converted through real life situations.[12] In God's design, conversion is an incarnational process.

Conversion and Relationships

By entering into relationships with "the other," living with them as neighbors and caring for them as family, the participants established relationships that were to change other relationships in their lives.

Conversion, according to Lonergan, is freely offered and initiates one into a share in God's life of relationship with all creation.[13] This invitation into God's life calls one into deeper relationship with self, others, and the cosmos. Wolski Conn's work on grace and sin in human growth provides insight into how there is already grace in the relational developments of life.[14]

Conversion and Compassion/Mercy

As the relationship between the participants and the refugees began to move beyond simple care into a relationship imbued with a quality of compassion or mercy, the participants began to feel the suffering of their neighbors. For Sobrino, "mercy is an attitude which works to eradicate suffering." [15]

Compassion/mercy and its capacity to move one to transcend service was striking for me during this process. It seems that the inbreaking of God in situations revealing loving compassion is as ancient as the Exodus story (Exod 3:7-8) and as contemporary as Darlene's experience of relating with Miriam. In each instance, liberation emerges from the heart of love.

In reflecting on Merton's conversion, Conn notes that at the heart of the Christian tradition, conversion is most recognized in "loving compassion," expressed in self-transcending human empathy and justice. Although I would never claim that the participants experienced the near total surrender of Merton, there were threads and themes of compassion and conversion that were a witness to it as discussed earlier.

Conversion and the Desire for Justice

Because of relationships of compassion/mercy, the participants began to reflect on the sources for the suffering of their neighbors. They began to analyze the causes of the injustices. At times, they felt as powerless and helpless as the refugees. However, the participants reflected together—and together moved beyond the powerlessness of their individual isolation. They prayed. They were moved to desire justice and then to act for justice. Together they experienced a sense of power, that they could do something, that they could make a difference. As they reached out in mercy, their desire for justice was kindled.

Conversion to Deeper Christian Love

During their action for justice, the vigil at Queen's Park, the participants knew that what they were doing might seem insignificant to others. They had to draw on a deeper power—the power of the spirit. They moved beyond ideologies of justice to a deeper faith perspective. They moved to a depth of love that encompassed suffering. They became closer companions of Christ, who carried a cross. Jesus became the parable of the participants' own conversion.

As Conn notes, in his "life, death and resurrection, Jesus lived out *the* Christian parable," and this is a challenge to "the ultimate religious conversion" for the Christian community.[16] As a remnant community of faith, I believe the participants in this study share in this challenge of conversion.

In his yearning for the Messiah and the prophets' call for the reign of God, Jesus represents the yearning of humankind. The participants were clear on their desire to know the presence of God as they tried to be about the kingdom of God. According to McFague, the preaching and way of life of Jesus were subversive and not what many thought God's chosen should say and do.[17] The participants continually sought wisdom and courage from the words and deeds of Jesus.

From his baptism and experience of God as *Abba*, Jesus' life and lifestyle were forever transformed. From Wainwright's work on the Gospel of Matthew, we know that Jesus enfleshed his new vision in compassion for those considered least by society. He prioritized this mission over the law of the Sabbath, and it led him to the cross, the ultimate parable in the Christian story.

In making choices for the marginalized of society, members of this reflection group often found themselves in anxious and threatening experiences. Each trip to the border with individuals or family members was a participation in the suffering of a fragile world. The cutbacks in resources were another cause of pain to their neighbors. For the participants, the image of the cross was not only a political symbol of how a society can crucify unwanted members, but a source of courage in the Parable of Jesus, the Christ. Hope in new life has become a principle of living for this group as they continue to struggle and participate in the mystery of Jesus as the parable of conversion.

THE PRINCIPLE OF CONVERSION

The dynamics involved in the Romero House theological project lead me to conclude that doing works of mercy can indeed carry one further into the process of ongoing conversion. Working for and with "the other" allows relationships to develop, compassion to deepen, and a desire for justice to thrive, as we are led into the deeper mystery of Christian love in the midst of suffering.

However, I was led to an even deeper insight. I began to see that mercy is not primarily about the "doing" of specific works. It is also an attitude, a horizon of being, or what Sobrino calls "a principle." According to him, "the principle of mercy" is "a fundamental attitude at the root of every human interaction," which then "affects all subsequent interactions." The principle of mercy gives priority to "mercy that becomes justice" by engaging all levels of energy: intellectual, religious, scientific, and technological.[18] Mercy is a principle that animates the whole process of ongoing conversion, leading one to a change in relationships, in thinking, in acting, and in believing.

Sobrino learned an amazing truth through the martyrdom of his brother Jesuits and the women who worked with them. He now believes that nothing is as "vital in order to live as a human being than to exercise mercy on behalf of crucified people, and that nothing is more humanizing than to believe in the God of Jesus."[19] This is a challenging belief in a world so crucified by unbalanced resources and faced with the martyrdom of terrorism.

From Sobrino's profound witness, and the simple reflections of the participants on their experience of mercy, I believe that it is in the doing of Mercy that one becomes merciful. In the exercise of this principle, mercy becomes a quality of being in the one who ministers. In doing mercy, one's being has the potential for entering into the process of Christian conversion at many levels.

The world is in desperate need of such mercy, for the principle of mercy enables us to place ourselves in situations and relationships that seem to require justice and often entail struggle or risk. How do we engage in such experiences? We may find ourselves contemplating the words of Scripture—"Who is my neighbor?"—or thinking about the ethical question—"What does love require?" In the dynamic of the principle of mercy, the questions and issues of justice are transformed into the questions and responses of love. As the pattern of the principle of mercy unfolds, we, like the disciples of the Gospel and the participants of the study, are led to the ultimate parable, the cross, of Jesus. Conn writes:

> The root of this transformed justice is the humility which Jesus, the model of true justice, calls his disciples to: loving service. . . . It is this loving service of the neighbor in the daily lives of his disciples that Jesus points to in the image of the cross: "If anyone wants to be a follower of mine, let them renounce themselves and take up the cross and follow me."[20]

It is in real situations of loving service and in responsible relationships with neighbors that authentic Christian conversion continues. In a global world our neighbors are often the "other," the one we do not recognize but who evokes the principle of mercy from the depths of our being.

Mary Atkins contemplates questions of neighbors and hospitality as the world witnesses a massive migration of peoples and the influx of strangers—to countries, to regions, to cities. She suggests that, in the tension between tolerance and hospitality, large societies may create just structures, but it is in small communities that strangers experience hospitality. Romero House is one such small community that has transcended tolerance and welcomed strangers with the hospitality of neighbors.[21]

REFLECTING ON EXPERIENCE

Six months following the initial project, the participants were asked to reflect on their experience of the theological reflection process. The responses are summarized below.

Elizabeth noted that the process helped her to realize how much Romero House contributed to her "emotional and spiritual growth." Further, she now finds that "in the middle of a meaningful or significant event" she will ask herself questions similar to those posed during the reflection process. Elizabeth believes that "doing the theological reflection process has helped [her] to really think and pray about these things."

Emile asserted that, since the theological reflection process and in particular the vigil, he has realized that he "does not want to do things and necessarily expect change but rather do them because they are right and of God." On the night of the vigil, the intent was not to change the government but only to do what the group valued and wanted to do in the name of God and justice.

Mary Jo believed that the process "provoked her to reflect/pray on what it means to be poor with the poor—to be in solidarity with the poor." She also noted that, since the process, she has changed "to the extent that it has changed us as a community." Mary Jo believes that the community "became disciples at the foot of the cross during the vigil—which now symbolizes where we are called during the day."

Winki realized that the reflection process helped her to "deepen [her] insights in the meaning of presence—as a member of a community." She has also become aware that "in a group process [she] is more alert to the potential significance of events that may be of bigger 'import' to those in the group, [herself] included."

Darlene knows that "articulating experience and reflecting on understanding always helps [her] to grow." She now feels "secure" in her faith but "struggles with living out [her] faith in the face of fears." Darlene believes that participating with "our reflection group has helped to lessen the fears."

Darlene appeared to grow in freedom and faith during the process, and her own words indicate how she experienced life after the process. "For a period of time, I experienced a real sense of joy and peace, a love for living and who I am. That is more or less strong from time to time but the blessing remains with me."

Shawn thinks that participating in the reflection process and "seeing the positive results of it really changed the way [he] practices 'discernment.'" Another insight for Shawn was that "before the sessions, [he] wasn't sold on the idea of the Holy Spirit really speaking through a group." He now has "a lot more faith" in group discernment, and he wants to try to "implement it more into [his] ministry" in the future.

Andrew continues to be more aware of the "presence of God in the social context" and wants to try to "bring some of what [he] learned into his work at the coalition for justice." It was important for Andrew that he experienced "a renewal in [his] spiritual life and in praying with the Scriptures." He now hopes that he and his wife can be a "mutual support in their spirituality," as they continue to work for justice and faith.

These reflections give witness to the grace of ongoing conversion and the principle of mercy alive in the experiences of the participants.

CONCLUSION

The principle of mercy, incarnate in the lives of ministers and of all members of the community of faith, is a living dynamic in the gift of ongoing conversion. To incarnate this principle is to live mercy and a response to the search for meaning in ministry.

Meaningful ministry is an important challenge in this world of globalization, characterized by the migration of peoples and an unstable neoliberal economy. When considering what vision can lead us as a community of Christians in ministry to be more committed to live the life, death, and resurrection of Jesus in this age of change, the image of a holy people in God's household from the letter to the Ephesians is worthy of reflection. We are reminded that we are no longer "strangers and aliens" of this land, but that together we are "citizens with the saints and also members of the household of God." We are called to be a community of faith built upon the foundations of the saints and prophets of old with Christ as the cornerstone. We are summoned to be a "dwelling place for God" in the Spirit (Eph 2:19, 22). Living the principle of mercy compels us to trust in this transforming work of the Spirit and minister in justice and love not as strangers but as neighbors.[22]

CONCLUSION

❖

THE SEARCH FOR MEANING IN MINISTRY

The search for meaning in ministry is ultimately the search for God, the reign of God, the vision of God. I believe that taking time to theologically reflect on experiences and praying to seek the presence of God in the complexities of life in church and society is an urgent call for all in ministry today. In this section we have explored the steps involved in this process of contemplating experiences in ministry, exploring the context of the events surrounding this experience, including what has become known as a social analysis; this critical analysis is followed by reflecting on the faith tradition of the minister, integrating the spirituality of the reflector, and discerning the next step in life or ministry. This transformative process becomes a meaningful practice for those I encounter in supervision and students integrating ministry with life and faith. Reflecting as a community of faith enhances the theological reflection process and the depth of meaning of those engaged in this shared reflection.

As mentioned earlier, many dedicated women and men in current ministry experience a form of ministry burnout sometimes called compassion fatigue. I believe the theological reflection process, especially practiced in a community setting, allows these ministers to take the necessary time to search for meaning, discern the sacred revealed in a given reality, and deepen their commitment of compassionate service and justice for the reign of God.

This reflective practice has the potential to lead one from task-driven ministry to ongoing conversion through the unfolding "principle of mercy." The staff of the Romero House community learned the transformative principle of mercy as they reflected on their practice of it within the Romero House community. They remained faithful to their relationships with the refugees even through the crisis of cutbacks by the government. Contemplating the essence of the cross, they gained courage to engage in the struggle for justice in this distressful reality. Ultimately, they discerned an ongoing commitment to be a community of love, where refugees were regarded as Gospel neighbors. Living the dynamic principle of mercy called them to ongoing conversion and gave meaning to a stressful ministry experience.

THEOLOGICAL REFLECTION AS INTEGRATION FOR MINISTRY

For close to ten years I have facilitated this transformative process of contemplative theological reflection in an academic setting in a program called Integration for Ministry. It has stood the test of time and a variety of experiences. Through this process, mature students, gathered as a community of faith, attempt to integrate their lives with their ministry experiences and theological studies. I am continually inspired by the willingness of these women and men to engage in this process of ongoing conversion. Guiding communities of students through this process has deepened my conviction of the value and importance of reflecting on personal and ministerial experience. To witness students making valiant, even "velvet" decisions about life and ministry is a wonder to behold. They experience the power of their growth in faith and trust through reflecting as a community of believers. One student revealed that this communal prayerful reflection process graced him with the courage to "change the scope of both the interior and outer world of my life." Along with others in this student community, the change he experienced gave him new energy for mission.

An imperative for quality practice in ministry is a quality theory of ministry grounded in a current theology. I shaped this contemplative process on tested theories of theological reflection and adult transformative learning. It is gratifying to realize that participants sensed the wisdom of these theories. An educator in the program experienced the process as a "sensitive and unyielding commitment to an adult pedagogical model that served not only to be instructive but also to be inspiring." He noted the transformative nature of the process "slowly overcame whatever ego-centered resistance threatened my learning." He did not stop but proclaimed a change in his practice of ministry, noting how grateful he was to "truly add another way of relating and ministering" to his life of service.

As the facilitator of this community of students, I have them participate in the following theological reflection processes:

- An experience of life, an event, story or narrative
- An experience of work or ministry, an event, story, or narrative
- An issue in ministry, justice, suffering, inculturation
- A vision of ministry, a personal mission statement

An Experience of Ministry

The transformative quality of a contemplative theological reflection has healing and empowering effects on the lives of those who gather as a community and reflect on experiences of ministry. In an honest reflection, one pastoral minister was freed to accept the painful realities of a former ministry experience, which was called "baggage." This process "enabled me to accept this baggage not only as part of my story but also to see myself in a story where even my blunders are part of an ongoing grace." The heart of this story was the hurt experienced, the reflection process that led to a deeper insight into the experience, and the challenge of "an obligation to seek reconciliation." By contemplatively and critically reflecting on this ministry experience, the context of a pastoral setting, faith in a theology of reconciliation and a spirituality of nonviolence, the pastoral minister was summoned to express a new "growth in freedom, faith, love and trust in God." This transformation was marked by an ongoing conversion from the reality of hurt to reconciliation.

An Issue of Ministry

Miriam: A minister reflecting on the issue of inculturation. Miriam (pseudonym) reflected on the issue of inculturation as she meditated on the "blessings and woes of our contemporary world." After many years of ministering in her homeland in South Africa, Miriam wanted to explore particular aspects of inculturation, especially the interaction between African culture and the Christian Gospel. She wanted to "engage in critical theological reflection and dialogue with my corner of the world and to search for how to best minister in that context." She especially wanted to reflect on how the Gospel can interact within the social and economic unrest of her local South African setting.

As she reflected on her experience of ministry, studied contextual theology, and reflected on her local culture, Miriam became more aware of how "culture influences theology." She also "saw the importance of reading the signs of the times to allow the gospel to critique the culture." Miriam reflected on both hopes and doubts in her local context. She sees the "Spirit at work in the midst of crisis" in the world, and has become aware of how this area of the world is influenced through such positive movements as interreligious dialogue, the Earth Charter, and justice groups working to eliminate world hunger.

Miriam discovered that great obstacles to "seeing and acting for justice are fear, apathy, indifference and blame-the-victim mentality." These dynamics and temptations are prevalent in her life and in her local community of faith. To help her confront her fear, Miriam learned to engage in contextual and social analysis; to ask such important questions as "Who benefits?" and "Who is burdened?" in every cultural and social situation. Miriam also came to recognize the "danger of extreme responses of cultures and religious traditions." New freedom came as she engaged her context of ministry more critically and honestly.

Miriam returns to her community with a new appreciation of the African culture and believing that "Christ and the gospel is the yardstick for critiquing culture." Her call to ongoing conversion was to move from inertia to embrace the challenges of the African culture and "collaborate with others in the guidance of the Holy Spirit in the work of promoting God's reign in the world." She now has renewed strength and energy for his mission, thanks to this time of reflection that resulted in "God breaking into (her) my life." Through this process Miriam is more convinced than ever that her ministry, faith, and spirituality are called to be "integrated with action for justice."

Hope, a midwife reflecting on the issue of suffering. A woman from the Caribbean, whom I will call Hope, worked as a pastoral minister and a midwife in her local area. She was particularly concerned with the suffering within her community and was aware that this suffering was indicative of the "plight of the world." Through the theological reflection process she found that "a new way of looking at reality emerged for me, especially in my attitude to suffering and pain in our world." Hope's theological reflection on suffering led her to contemplate the cross and the passion of Christ. Her meditation is simple and wise. It has a liberating tone and resonates with a quality of one who knows suffering and the reality of the cross from the "underside." She comments:

> To contemplate the Passion does not mean that I dwell on the gore of Mel Gibson. It does not mean that I expect God to grant an immediate rescue squad or relief; neither does it mean instant paradise, transfiguration or glory. There is no shortcut to glory. I need to discover over and over again the work of God in the Passion, suffering and death of Christ. . . . The deeper meaning of the passion is situated in God's whole act of creation, incarnation and salvation.

Hope's reflection led her to the belief that "the whole of life" is a series of deaths and rebirths; just as her ministry as a midwife led her to reflect on the ebb and flow of life and death. She now understands ministry as living the "mystery of Christ's life, death, and resurrection," and chooses to return to her community in solidarity with all who live and suffer through life's events. As she reflected on the suffering of others, life and birth became one evolving movement:

> Suffering is not like a nine month's pregnancy that a woman endures, goes through labor, gives birth and it is over. We become embryos over and over again until we are swept through life events and into eternal birth and glory.

As Hope reflected on her ministry experience, she began to see herself as "a disciple in our contemporary world," and she became conscious of a call "to join God in the mission of birthing and bringing about new life."

Hope believes that theological reflection gave her a new way to contemplate the paschal mystery: this "process has helped me to understand ministry better as God's project in our world." Hope acknowledges that "God has enlarged my vision to see what can be done in what seemed initially to me as a desperate situation." Her new vision of ministry is participating in the reality of God's whole act of creation, incarnation, and salvation.

A Vision of Ministry

Students in the Integration for Ministry program are challenged to reflect on a vision of ministry that will inspire a ministerial response despite the immensity of any issue on a given day. Students are asked to contemplate their mission and seek therein a depth of vision that has the potential to reveal an understanding that will summon them to imagine a merciful and just response to issues in their ministry or work. They are encouraged to consider what inspires that clear or deep emotion that reveals their commitment to this mission. It is a wonder to see the vision for mission present in those involved in both ecclesial and nonecclesial settings.

One way to help focus such a reflection is to have the students compose a personal mission statement. In this setting I encourage the student to use the flow of the theological reflection process as a possible outline for their vision of ministry. The personal mission statements include:

- personal identity
- context of mission (worldview)
- theological statement of mission
- spirituality of mission
- ongoing call to transformation

A Canadian businessman came to our program to refocus his Christian identity and professional calling, his ministry in the marketplace. This contemplative approach to theological reflection led him to integrate his life with his spiritual search for meaning. His mission statement, printed below, reveals a person involved in leadership in his workplace in the multicultural city of Toronto and other areas of the world. As he encounters his contemporaries in work, society, and church settings, he meets persons from multiple faiths who often reveal their spiritual journeys. He feels a deep call to support those he encounters. He is grounded in his Christian identity while respectful of the diverse faiths of those he meets along the way.

Mission Statement

My objective for ministry is to help people find wholeness in their lives by integrating their spiritual journey with the various realities of their existence: culture, education, commerce, community, and family. I will serve my community as necessary, providing companionship, support, leadership, and teaching to those who may seek God while facing the struggles and joys of earthly life. My ministry will be primarily built on a Christian foundation and a Catholic tradition. However, I will work both within the institutional church as well as the broader context, endeavoring to minister to people from all walks of life and varying religious beliefs.

This professional man is committed as a Catholic Christian to the ministry of supporting others on their spiritual journey in his local and international communities.

TRANSFORMATIVE COMPETENCIES FOR MINISTRY

Theological reflection practiced in a setting of ministerial formation challenges students to become both compassionate and competent in the practice of ministry. One way to look at this is through the lens of transformative competencies for ministry. Noted below are several examples that, in my experience of facilitating theological reflection, I have found led to ongoing conversion and the principle of mercy.

A Process of Ongoing Conversion
in Relationships with God, Self, and Others:

- Capacity for discernment in reality and in relationships in ministry
- Participation in a community of worship and ministry
- Ability to engage theological reflection processes
- Knowledge and practice of interpersonal skills
- Contribution to collaborative efforts in ministry situation
- Willingness to be mentored in ministry

The Principle of Mercy:

- Willingness for ministry placement in service with others
- Potential to be moved in a work of mercy by a spirit of compassion evoked from another
- Ability to maintain responsible relationships in difficult situations
- Desire and capability in working for community and justice
- Knowledge and appreciation of a sound theology of the cross
- Contribution to a gospel vision of Christian love

I have sought in this book to describe the essential parts of a working model of contemplative theological reflection: Contemplating the Experience, Exploring the Context, Reflecting on the Religious Tradition, and Integrating Spirituality. A decision to respond to a summons to ongoing conversion is the fruit of integrating these critical and contemplative reflections. The roots of this process can be seen in the works of James and Evelyn Whitehead and Mary Ellen Sheehan; however, this model values contemplative prayer as a significant feature of the process, and I believe this practice contributed to the transformative quality of the decisions made by these participants.

CONTEMPLATIVE THEOLOGICAL REFLECTION PROCESS AND JOURNALING

The contemplative theological reflection process I designed includes time for prayer, reflective journaling, faith sharing and dialogue, discernment and celebration. I encourage participants to bring their own experience and critical information about a story or topic for theological reflection. In most cases, the process takes place over an extended number of meetings, usually four or five gatherings, of at least two hours each.

At each gathering, after socializing for a while, we take time for prayer and quiet to support participants in contemplating an experience, a story, and to seek the work of God in their lives. This same experience or story is brought to each gathering, and time is spent contemplating the other sources of reflection surrounding the experience—context, tradition, and spirituality—to discern God's continuous summons to ongoing conversion.

Journaling is a helpful process to record reflections that are both contemplative and critical. To assist the participants of this process, I created a series of journal sheets to be used by participants after each period of prayerful reflection (appendix 1). These journal sheets were helpful for participants to record their reflections and were also important as they shared their faith and dialogued about their experience of theological reflection. The participants were strongly encouraged to disclose only what they freely wished to share. Participants reported that praying, journaling together in quiet, and sharing reflections in community, helped them to grow in trust that God was present in their experience and in feeling less alone in their situation.

Integration, or the coming together of these reflections, is as unique as there are individual participants.

It is my deepest desire that through the practice of contemplative theological reflection as presented here, to ministers and people of good faith, they will have the wisdom and strength to respond effectively to the decisions the church and global communities need. Through this process I believe many will be transformed by the tender love of God already at work in our world.

Appendix 1

CONTEMPLATIVE
THEOLOGICAL REFLECTION JOURNAL

❖

1. Reflection on Experience in Ministry

Suggested Scripture for Contemplation:

The woman said to him, "I know that Messiah is coming" (who is called Christ). "When he comes, he will proclaim all things to us." Jesus said to her, "I am he, the one who is speaking to you." (John 4:25-26)

Jesus said to his disciples:
"As the Father has loved me, so I have loved you; abide in
      my love.
. . . You did not choose me but I chose you." (John 15:9, 16)

Journal Questions:

Focus on an experience that has the potential to reveal to you a depth of value in your ministry or work. It would be well to consider an experience that holds some clear or deep emotion for you. Try to frame this experience as a question or as a statement of your ministry incorporating the five Ws (who, what, when, why, where).

Name at least two feelings you undergo as you reflect on this experience in ministry.

Name any insight or understanding that comes to you as you reflect on this experience in ministry.

Name or draw an image that captures the heart of the matter of this reflection on your experience in ministry.

Expectations:
Name any hopes or desires you have in light of this reflection on ministry.

2. Reflection on the Context of Experience in Ministry

Suggested Scripture for Contemplation:
If you make my word your home, you will indeed be my
   disciples.
You will learn the truth, and the truth will set you free. (John
   8:31, my translation)

Journal Questions:
The goal of this reflection is to evoke conversation between the context (your view of the world/universe, creation, movements, political and/or social realities, location, trends, the arts, cultural values, folklore, interpersonal relations, etc.) within which your ministry takes place, and your recalled ministry experience. How does the context speak with your reflections on this experience?

Social Analysis Question:
In this context, who benefits and who is burdened?

Expectations:
Name any hopes, desires, doubts, questions, or decisions that
   are emerging from this reflection.

3. Reflection on Faith Tradition and Experience in Ministry

Suggested Scripture for Contemplation:
I do not call you servants any longer, because the servant does not know what the master is doing; but I have called you friends, because I have made known to you everything revealed to me through my relationship with God. (John 15:15, my translation)

Journal Questions:

The goal here is to evoke conversation between tradition and experience in ministry.

How did/does the Christian tradition (Sacred Scripture, sacraments, saints and prophets, truths, Wisdom, teachings of faith, Christian heritage, social justice documents, etc.), speak with your experience of ministry? How did/do such theological themes as God, Jesus, mercy, creation, grace, sin, church, redemption, conversion, justice, mysteries of the faith, incarnation, ministry, etc., figure into your "conversation"?

Expectations:

Name any hopes, desires, doubts, questions, or decisions that are beginning to emerge as you reflect on this conversation between tradition and your ministry experience.

4. Reflection on Spirituality and Experience in Ministry

Suggested Scripture for Contemplation:

Make your home in me, as I make mine in you. As a branch cannot bear fruit all by itself, but must remain part of the vine, neither can you unless you remain in me. I am the vine, you are the branches. (John 15:4-5, my translation)

Journal Questions:

The goal of this reflection is to evoke conversation between your lived spirituality and your experience of ministry.

How does your lived spirituality speak with your experience in ministry?

How does your experience in ministry relate to your spirituality:

> Your life of faith in everyday experience;
> The gift of your relationship with God revealed in Christ
> by the power of the Holy Spirit;

> Your life lived in a community of giving and receiving love with God, with others, within yourself and with the cosmos?

Expectations:
Name any hopes, desires, doubts, questions, or decisions that are beginning to emerge from this reflection on ministry and spirituality.

5. Integration of Experience in Ministry with Context, Tradition, and Spirituality

Suggested Scripture for Contemplation:
God, who is rich in mercy, out of the great love with which we are loved, even when we were dead through our trespasses, made us alive together with Christ. . . . For by grace you have been saved through faith; and this is not your own doing, it is the gift of God—not because of works, lest anyone should boast. For *we are God's work of art*, created in Christ Jesus for good works, which God prepared beforehand, that we should walk in them. (Eph 2:4-10, my translation)

Journal Questions:
The goal of this reflective exercise is to evoke integration of ministry with context, tradition, and spirituality—integration that includes a process of discernment and a response.

In your reflections, what similarities did you notice in the tradition, context, and spirituality of your experience of ministry?

In your reflections, what differences did you notice in the tradition, context, and spirituality of your experience in ministry?

What do these similarities and differences reveal to you?

Expectations:
How have your initial, or emerging, expectations/hopes or doubts been challenged or confirmed?

Can you name any insight or understanding about your questions or doubts that have come from this reflection?

Response
Is there a judgment and/or decision you feel called to make after reflecting on this experience of ministry?

Is there a new discernment or a call to ongoing conversion from this reflection?

Celebration
What prayerful symbol (ordinary article, poem, piece of music or artwork, etc.) best ritualizes a growth in faith, ongoing conversion or transformation, that brings you to this response? This symbol is shared at the closing ritual prayer, a celebration of gratitude.

Appendix 2

A WORKING MODEL OF CONTEMPLATIVE THEOLOGICAL REFLECTION[1]

❖

Step 1. *Contemplation on an experience of the reality of life in an event, issue, or story to discern God's presence and call to ongoing conversion:*
who, what, where, when, how, feelings, insights, understanding, meaning . . . an image that captures the heart of the matter from contemplating this experience.

Step 2. *Contemplation and consideration of participant's expectations:*

hopes, desires, doubts and questions . . .

Step 3. *Other sources for contemplation and critical consideration:*

A. Context:

critical view of the culture, the world/universe, creation, movements, political and/or social reality, location, trends, cultural values, folklore, interpersonal relations, as they relate to the participant's experience, etc.

Social Analysis Question:
In this context, who benefits and who is burdened?

B. *Tradition:*

Sacred Scripture, social justice teachings, truths, Wisdom and teachings of faith, Christian heritage, the saints and prophetic figures, theological themes (e.g., creation, grace, sin, redemption, conversion, image of God . . .)

C. *Spirituality:*

Consider spirit, mind, body, and creation.

(1) lived experience of the presence or absence of God
(2) lived relationship with God and resistance to God
(3) integration of life with Faith vision, e.g.,
     (a) life of simplicity and identification with the poor
     (b) service and the gospel invitation of discipleship
     (c) consumerism and a vision of money as a god

Step 4. *Sources in critical and reflective conversation with each other*

Step 5. *Expectations reviewed:*
hopes, desires, doubts, questions, etc.

Step 6. *Prayerful consideration of the above; discernment of response*

Step 7. *Celebration and Ritual of Gratitude for call to ongoing conversion*

A MODEL OF CONTEMPLATIVE THEOLOGICAL REFLECTION
START WITH

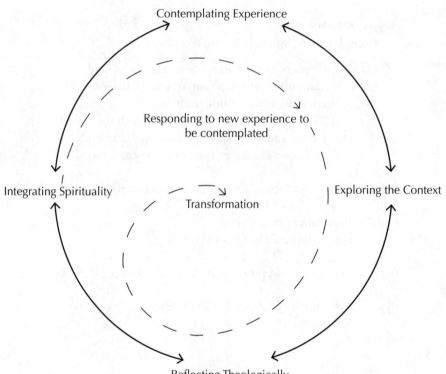

Contemplating Experience

Responding to new experience to
be contemplated

Integrating Spirituality

Transformation

Exploring the Context

Reflecting Theologically

Contemplating experience: A story or issue from experience, which causes you/us to rethink and pray about deeper truths and values.

Exploring the context: How does the context (the surrounding situation) of this story contribute to or challenge your/our interpretation of this experience?

> *Social analysis question:*
> In this context, who benefits and who is burdened?

Reflecting theologically: From the faith tradition, what Scripture story or mystery in the Christian tradition contributes to or challenges your/our interpretation of this experience?
Where and how is God active in this experience?

Integrating spirituality: What truths, values, or actions does this interpretation call forth from your/our internalized vision of faith?
Is there a new discernment or a call to ongoing conversion from this reflection?

NOTES

Introduction—pp. 1–4

1. T. S. Eliot, "The Dry Savages," in *T. S. Eliot's Collected Poems, 1909–1996* (Orlando, FL: Harcourt Brace, 1963), 191–200.

2. For further information about Romero House see www.romerohouse. org/.

Chapter 1—pp. 7–11

1. Joseph A. Komonchak, Mary Collins, and Dermot A. Lane, eds., *The New Dictionary of Theology* (Collegeville: Liturgical Press, 1993), s.v. "Ministry," by Thomas F. O'Meara, OP.

2. Albert Nolan, OP, "Contextual Theology: One Faith, Many Theologies," Chancellor's Address at Regis College, Toronto, Ontario, 1990, 18.

3. Sandra Schneiders, *What Is Theology? What Ever Happened to the One Right Answer?* Video, 1995.

4. Thomas O'Meara, *Theology of Ministry* (New York: Paulist Press), 15.

5. Brian O. McDermott, SJ, "The Relationship Among Authority, Leadership, and Spirituality in Ministry," in Robert Wicks, ed., *Handbook of Spirituality for Ministers* (New York: Paulist Press, 1995), 388.

6. John C. Haughey, "The Role of Prayer in Action/Reflection Groups," in *Tracing the Spirit* (New York: Paulist Press, 1983), 119.

7. Mary Ellen Sheehan, "Theological Reflection and Theory-Praxis Integration: An Experience with the Case Study Method," *Pastoral Studies* 3 (1984): 32.

Chapter 2—pp. 12–27

1. James D. Whitehead and Evelyn Eaton Whitehead, *Method in Ministry: Theological Reflection and Christian Ministry* (New York: The Seabury Press, 1980), 11–26.

2. Mary Ellen Sheehan, "Theological Reflection and Theory-Praxis Integration: An Experience with the Case Study Method," *Pastoral Studies* 3 (1984): 25–38.

3. Mary Ellen Sheehan, "Social Sciences and Theology: Mutually Necessary Conversation Partners" (Monroe, MI: Festival Papers of IHM Theology Conference, 1995).

4. David J. Bosch, *Transforming Mission: Paradigm Shifts in Theology of Mission* (New York: Orbis Books, 1991), 33. See also, Stephan B. Bevans and Roger P. Schroeder, *Constants and Context: A Theology of Mission for Today* (New York: Orbis Books, 2004).

5. Whitehead and Whitehead, *Method in Ministry*, 96–97. For a now classical review of the method of correlating questions of culture and a response of theology, see Paul Tillich, *Systematic Theology: Reason and Revelation*, vol. 1. (Chicago: University of Chicago Press, 1973), 60.

6. Jack Mezirow, "Transformation Theory," presentation at the Adult Education Research Conference Proceedings, Calgary, Alberta, Canada (May 6–8, 1988), 227.

7. Ibid.

8. Ibid., 117.

9. Donald A. Schon, *Educating the Reflective Practitioner* (San Francisco: Jossey-Bass, 1987), 13.

10. Ibid., 35.

11. John P. Miller, *The Contemplative Practitioner: Meditation in Education and the Professions* (Toronto: OISE Press, 1994), 122.

12. For a further study of professionalism in ministry, see Maureen F. McDonnell, "The Tension Between the Professional and Vocational Dimensions of Spiritual Direction Ministry: A Contemporary Challenge Facing the Supervisor of Spiritual Directors," Doctor of Ministry thesis, The University of Toronto, The Toronto School of Theology, 2005.

13. Schon, *Educating the Reflective Practitioner*, 35.

Chapter 3—pp. 31–63

1. Tad Dunne, *Lonergan and Spirituality: Towards a Spiritual Integration* (Chicago: Loyola University Press, 1985), 177.

2. It is interesting to note how these participants now generously contribute to society. Within a few years of ending this process, Winki retired from nursing and continues to volunteer at Romero House. Shawn became an Anglican priest and serves a First Nations Community working for justice concerns in Saskatoon. He is married and is now a father. Darlene is now a theologian, specializing in Catholic Social Ethics for economic justice and sustainability. She is executive director of Galilee Center, Arnprior, Ontario, where she promotes holistic development, justice, and ecology. Andrew and his wife moved to the Romero House neighborhood and he is now a father and a refugee lawyer. He supervises test cases as cochair of the Legal Affairs Committee of the Canadian Council of Refugees. Elizabeth

became an International Lawyer, serves the needs of refugees, advocates for housing for the elderly, and is married with two children. Mary Jo continues as director of the Romero House community, teaches courses in contextual spirituality and justice at Regis College, and lectures at various universities and public forums throughout North America. Emile is now married and continues to address the concerns of refugees as he contributes his experience and skills at The Francophone Centre in Toronto.

3. Walter Conn, *Christian Conversion: A Developmental Interpretation of Autonomy and Surrender* (New York: Paulist Press, 1986), 193.

4. Ibid., 200.

5. Donald L. Gelpi, SJ, "The Dynamics of Personal Conversion," in *Inculturating North American Theology* (Atlanta: Scholars Press, 1988), 33.

6. For the stories of the refugees connected with this theological reflection process, read Mary Jo Leddy, *At the Border Called Hope: Where Refugees Are Neighbours* (Toronto: Harper Collins, 1997).

Chapter 4—pp. 64–75

1. Robert J. Schreiter, "Plurality and Difference in an Unstable World," lecture given January 24, 2004, at the Scarborough Mission Center in Toronto. For further information on Schreiter's development of contextual theology, see Robert J. Schreiter, *Constructing Local Theologies* (Maryknoll, NY: Orbis Books, 2002).

2. Robert Schreiter, "A New Modernity: Living and Believing in an Unstable World," the 2005 Anthony Jordan Lectures, Newman Theological College, Edmonton, Alberta, March 18–19, 2005, 1–3.

3. Ibid., 3.

4. Ibid., 25.

5. Ibid., 3.

6. Shashank Bengali, "Nigeria teems with people evicted from homes," Knight Rider Newspaper, carried by the *Detroit Free Press*, February 16, 2006, sec. A, p. 1.

7. Schreiter, "A New Modernity," 3.

8. Ibid., 4.

9. Ibid., 12.

10. Ibid., 34.

11. Article 1, The 1951 *Convention Relating to the Status of Refugees*, United Nations High Commissioner for Refugees, www.unhcr.org (accessed September 15, 2008).

12. Primarily because of the terrorist attacks of September 11, 2001, on the United States, and also because of an increase in terrorism around the globe, some nation-states have tightened their immigration regulations. This has had a serious, negative impact on the acceptance rates for many refugees. Infoplease

.com, "Countries Hosting Refugees, 2006." http://www.infoplease.com/ipa/A0931917.html (accessed September 15, 2008). Another important article supporting this information is: United Nations High Commission on Refugees, "The State of the World's Refugees 2006." http://www.unhcr.org/publ/PUBL/4444d3c220.html (accessed September 15, 2008).

13. Canadian Border Services Agency, "Safe Third Country Agreement." http://www.cbsa-asfc.gc.ca/agency/stca-etps-eng.html (accessed September 16, 2008).

14. Michael Swan, "Safe Third Country Agreement Challenged by Churches" (Canadian Christianity, 2008). http://www.canadianchristianity.com/nationalupdates/080828third.html (accessed September 16, 2008).

15. Schreiter, "A New Modernity," 31.

16. Mary Jo Leddy, *At the Border Called Hope: Where Refugees Are Neighbours* (Toronto: HarperCollins, 1997), 285–86.

17. Ibid., 286.

18. Douglas John Hall, *Thinking the Faith: Christian Theology in a North American Context* (Minneapolis: Fortress Press, 1991), 159.

19. Thomas Walkom, "State of the Right," The Star, 5 April, 1997, sec A, pp. 1, 21.

20. Hall, *Thinking the Faith*, 45.

21. Ibid., 177.

22. Ibid., 25.

23. Ibid., 74.

24. Wolkam, "State of the Right," A, 5.

25. Bob Holmes, "Following Jesus at a Distance: A Lenten Reflection on Discipleship," *The Mustard Seed*, Lent, 1997, 5.

26. Ibid., 5.

27. Annual Report for 2007 of the Canadian Association of Food Banks, 1–2; http://cafb-acba.ca/documents/2007AnnualReport(EnglishB).pdf.

28. Walkom, "State of the Right," A. 5.

29. Ibid., A, 5.

Chapter 5—pp. 76–98

1. Michael Crosby, "The Biblical Vision of Conversion," in *The Human Experience of Conversion: Persons and Structures in Transformation*, ed. Francis A. Eigo, O.S.A. (Villanova: Villanova University Press, 1987), 45.

2. Edward Schillebeeckx, *Jesus* (New York: Seabury Press, 1979), 224.

3. Ibid., 47.

4. Donald P. Gray, "Was Jesus a Convert?" *Religion in Life* 43 (Winter 1974): 449; citing Hugh Montefiore, *Awkward Questions on Christian Love* (Philadelphia: Westminster Press, 1964), 455.

5. Demetrius Dumm, *Flowers in the Desert: A Spirituality of the Bible* (New York: Paulist Press, 1987), 28.

6. Gray, "Was Jesus a Convert?" 449.

7. Ibid., 449.

8. Elaine Wainwright, "The Gospel of Matthew," in *Searching the Scriptures: A Feminist Commentary*, ed. Elisabeth Schüssler Fiorenza (New York: Crossroad, 1994), 636.

9. Ibid., 637.

10. Jon Sobrino, *Christology at the Crossroads* (New York: Orbis Books, 1978), 92.

11. Wainwright, "The Gospel of Matthew," 637.

12. Dom Marc-Francois Lacon, "Conversion and Kingdom in the Synoptic Gospels" in *Conversion: Perspectives on Personal and Social Transformation*, ed. Walter E. Conn (New York: Paulist Press, 1978), 115–18.

13. Jon Sobrino, *The Principle of Mercy: Taking the Crucified People from the Cross* (New York: Orbis Books, 1994) 15–26.

14. Sally McFague, "Conversion: Life on the Edge of the Raft," *Interpretation* 32, no.3 (July 78): 258.

15. Bernard J. F. Lonergan, *Method in Theology* (Toronto: University of Toronto Press, 1971), 105.

16. Karl Barth, "The Awakening to Conversion," in *Conversion: Perspectives on Personal and Social Transformation*, ed. Walter E. Conn (New York: Paulist Press, 1987), 35–50.

17. Joanne Wolski Conn, *Spirituality and Personal Maturity* (New York: Paulist Press, 1989), 3.

18. Elizabeth Johnson, *She Who Is: The Mystery of God in Feminist Theological Discourse* (New York: Crossroad, 1993), 64.

19. Valerie Saiving, "The Human Situation: A Feminine View," in *Womanspirit Rising*, eds. Carol Christ and Judith Plaskow (San Francisco: Harper and Row, 1979), 41.

20. Joseph A. Komonchak, Mary Collins, and Dermot A. Lane, eds., *The New Dictionary of Theology* (Collegeville: Liturgical Press, 1993), s.v. "Sin," by William E. May, 957.

21. John Macmurray, *Reason and Emotion* (London: Faber and Faber, 1936), 35.

22. Lonergan, *Method*, 241.

23. Bernard Lonergan, "Theology in Its New Context," in *Conversion: Perspectives on Personal and Social Transformation*, ed. Walter E. Conn (New York: Paulist Press, 1987), 13.

24. Ibid., 14.

25. Ibid.; emphasis mine.

26. Dean Brackley, *The Call to Discernment in Troubled Times: New Perspectives on the Transformative Wisdom of Ignatius of Loyola* (New York: Crossroad,

2004), 168–69. Also, "Higher Standards for Higher Education: The Christian University and Solidarity," http://www.creighton.edu/CollaborativeMinistry/brackley.html.

27. Ibid., 13–14.

28. Donald L. Gelpi, *The Turn to Experience in Contemporary Theology* (New York: Paulist Press, 1994), 134.

29. Walter Conn, *Christian Conversion: A Developmental Interpretation of Autonomy and Surrender* (New York: Paulist Press, 1986), 268.

30. Karl Rahner, "Conversion," in *The Concise Sacramentum Mundi* (New York: Seabury Press, 1975), 291–95.

31. Ibid., 293.

32. Douglas John Hall, *Thinking the Faith: Christian Theology in a North American Context* (Minneapolis: Fortress Press, 1991), 26–27; quoting Abraham Heschel.

33. Ibid., 26–27. Note: Although I value inclusive language I will respect direct quotations from primary sources, as in this letter of Dietrich Bonhoeffer.

34. Elizabeth Johnson, "Redeeming the Name of Christ," in *Freeing Theology: The Essential of Theology in Feminist Perspective*, ed. Catherine Mowry LaCugna (San Francisco: Harper Collins, 1993), 124.

35. Margaret Brennan, "Historical Consciousness: Ecclesial and Congregational Reflections" (Monroe, MI: Festival Papers of IHM Theology Conference, 1995), 2.

36. Elizabeth A. Johnson, "Redeeming the Name of Christ," in *Freeing Theology: The Essential of Theology in Feminist Perspective* (San Francisco, Harper Collins, 1993), 123.

37. Ibid., 124.

38. Edmund Arens, *Christopraxis: A Theology of Action* (Minneapolis: Fortress Press, 1995), 41–49.

39. Ibid., 62.

40. Elisabeth Schüssler Fiorenza, *Discipleship of Equals: A Critical Ekklesiaology of Liberation* (New York: Crossroad, 1993), 12.

41. Arens, *Christopraxis*, 15.

42. Avery Dulles, *Models of the Church* (New York: Doubleday, 1987); and *A Church to Believe In: Discipleship and the Dynamics of Freedom* (New York: Crossroad, 1982).

43. "Clergy," in Freidrich Gerhard, ed., Geoffrey W. Bromily, trans., *Theological Dictionary of the New Testament* (Grand Rapids, MI: Eerdmans, 1968).

44. Joseph A. Komonchak, Mary Collins, and Dermot A. Lane, eds., *The New Dictionary of Theology* (Collegeville: Liturgical Press, 1993), s.v. "Ministry," by Thomas F. O'Meara, OP.

45. David Tracy, "Theology and the Many Faces of Postmodernity," *Theology Today* 51, no. 1 (April 1994): 220.

46. Ibid., 108.

Chapter 6—pp. 99–111

1. Joann Wolski Conn, "Toward Spiritual Maturity," in *Freeing Theology: The Essential of Theology in Feminist Perspective*, ed. Catherine Mowry LaCugna (San Francisco: Harper Collins, 1993), 237.

2. Irene Nowell, "Mercy," in *New Dictionary of Theology* (Collegeville, MN: Liturgical Press, 1993), 650.

3. Jeanne Stevenson Moessner, "A New Pastoral Paradigm and Practice," in *Women in Travail and Transition*, eds. Maxine Glaz and Jeanne Stevenson Moessner (Minneapolis: Fortress Press, 1991), 202.

4. Ibid.

5. Jon Sobrino, *The Principle of Mercy: Taking the Crucified People from the Cross* (New York: Orbis Books, 1994), 1–20.

6. Maria Clara Bingemer, "Women in the Future of the Theology of Liberation," in *Expanding the View*, ed. Marc H. Ellis (New York: Orbis Books, 1990), 186–87.

7. Walter Conn, ed., *Conversion: Perspectives on Personal and Social Transformation* (New York: Paulist Press, 1978), 258.

8. Thomas Merton, "Seeds of Contemplation," in *A Thomas Merton Reader*, ed. Thomas P. McDonnell (Garden City, NY: Doubleday Image, 1974 [1962]), 426, 429.

9. Thomas Merton, *Conjectures of a Guilty Bystander* (Toronto: Doubleday, 1968), 156.

10. Richard Rohr and Joseph Martos, *The Wild Man's Journey: Reflections on Male Spirituality* (Cincinnati, OH: St. Anthony Messenger Press, 1992), 164–65.

11. Karl Rahner, "Conversion," in Conn, *Conversion: Perspectives on Personal and Social Transformation*, 204.

12. Rohr and Martos, *The Wild Man's Journey*, 164–65.

13. Bernard Lonergan, "Theology in Its New Context," in *Conversion: Perspectives on Personal and Social Transformation*, 12–15.

14. Joanne Wolski Conn, *Spirituality and Personal Maturity*, (New York: Paulist Press, 1989), 1–34.

15. Sobrino, *Principle of Mercy*, 18.

16. Walter Conn, *Christian Conversion: A Developmental Interpretation of Autonomy and Surrender* (New York: Paulist Press, 1986), 214.

17. Sally McFague, "Conversion: Life on the Edge of the Raft," *Interpretation* 32, no. 3 (July 1978): 258.

18. Sobrino, *Principle of Mercy*, 10.

19. Ibid., 11.

20. Conn, *Conversion*, 203.

21. Mary Atkins, "Who Is My Neighbour? Justice and Hospitality in a World of Strangers," lecture at the Catholic Theological Association in Leeds,

September 2004, http://www.cafod.org.uk/resources/worship/theological_articles/who_is_my_neighbour (accessed March 31, 2006).

22. Robert Schreiter, "A New Modernity: Living and Believing in an Unstable World," The 2005 Anthony Jordan Lectures, Newman Theological College, Edmonton, Alberta, March 18–19, 2005, 35.

Appendix 2

1. By "contemplative" I am not referring to a deep mystical experience, but rather the kind of relationship with God in which you are able to notice what God is like and what God is doing, be affected by it, notice how one is affected, and respond to God out of that awareness. Brian O. McDermott, SJ, "The Relationship Among Authority, Leadership, and Spirituality in Ministry," in Robert Wicks, ed., *Handbook of Spirituality for Ministers* (New York: Paulist Press, 1995), 388.

BIBLIOGRAPHY

❖

Arens, Edmund. *Christopraxis: A Theology of Action.* Translated by John F. Hoffmeyer. Minneapolis: Fortress Press, 1995.

Atkins, Mary. "Who Is My Neighbour? Justice and Hospitality in a World of Strangers." Lecture at the Catholic Theological Association in Leeds, September 2004, http://www.cafod.org.uk/resources/worship/theological_articles/who_is_my_neighbour (accessed March 31, 2008).

Barth, Karl. "The Awakening to Conversion." In *Conversion: Perspectives on Personal and Social Transformation,* edited by Walter E. Conn. New York: Paulist Press, 1987.

Bengali, Shashank. "Nigeria teems with people evicted from homes." *Detroit Free Press,* February 16, 2006, sec. A.

Bevans, Stephan B., and Roger P. Schroeder. *Constants and Context: A Theology of Mission for Today.* New York: Orbis Books, 2004.

Bingemer, Maria Clara. "Women in the Future of the Theology of Liberation." In *Expanding the View,* edited by Marc H. Ellis. New York: Orbis Books, 1990.

Bosch, David J. *Transforming Mission: Paradigm Shifts in Theology of Mission.* New York: Orbis Books, 1991.

Brackley, Dean. *The Call to Discernment in Troubled Times: New Perspective on the Transformative Wisdom of Ignatius of Loyola.* New York: Crossroad, 2004.

———. *Higher Standards for Higher Education: The Christian University and Solidarity,* http://www.creighton.edu/CollaborativeMinistry/brackley.html (accessed April 10, 2006).

Brennan, Margaret. "Historical Consciousness: Ecclesial and Congregational Reflections." *Festival Papers: IHM Theology Conference.* Monroe, MI: August 1995.

Canadian Association of Food Banks. *Annual Report for 2004 of the Canadian Association of Food Banks*, 3, http://cafb-acba.ca/documents/07annual_report.pdf (accessed September 15, 2008).

Canadian Border Services Agency. *Safe Third Country Agreement*. http://www.cbsa-asfc.gc.ca/agency/stca-etps-eng.html (accessed September 16, 2008).

Carr, Anne E. *Transforming Grace: Christian Tradition and Women's Experience*. San Francisco: Harper and Row, 1988.

Clark, Corita. *A Spirituality for Active Ministry*. Kansas City, MO: Sheed and Ward, 1991.

Clark, Thomas E. "A New Way: Reflecting on Experience." In *Tracing the Spirit*, edited by James Hug. New York: Paulist Press, 1993.

Conn, Walter. *Conversion: Perspectives on Personal and Social Transformation*. New York: Alba House, 1978.

———. *Christian Conversion: A Developmental Interpretation of Autonomy and Surrender*. New York: Paulist Press, 1986.

Crosby, Michael. "The Biblical Vision of Conversion" in *The Human Experience of Conversion: Persons and Structures in Transformation*, edited by Francis A. Eigo. Villanova: Villanova University Press, 1987.

Dulles, Avery. *A Church to Believe In: Discipleship and the Dynamics of Freedom*. New York: Crossroad, 1982.

———. *Models of the Church*. Expanded edition. New York: Doubleday, 1987.

Dumm, Demetrius. *Flowers in the Desert: A Spirituality of the Bible*. New York: Paulist Press, 1987.

Dunne, Tad. *Lonergan and Spirituality: Towards a Spiritual Integration*. Chicago: Loyola University Press, 1985.

Eliot, T. S. *T. S. Eliot's Collected Poems, 1909–1996*. Orlando, FL: Harcourt Brace, 1963.

Gelpi, Donald. *Inculturating North American Theology: An Experiment in Foundational Method*. Atlanta: Scholars Press, 1988.

———. *The Turn to Experience in Contemporary Theology*. New York: Paulist Press, 1994.

Gerhard, Freidrich, ed. *Theological Dictionary of the New Testament*. Translated by Geoffrey W. Bromily. Grand Rapids, MI: Eerdmans, 1968, s.v. "Clergy."

Gray, Donald P. "Was Jesus a Convert?" *Religion in Life* 43 (Winter 1974): 445–55.

Griffin, Emilie. *Turning: Reflections on the Experience of Conversion.* New York: Image Books, 1982.

Griffin, Virginia. "Holistic Learning / Teaching in Adult Education: Would You Play a One-String Guitar?" In *Appreciating Adult Learning: From the Learners' Perspective,* edited by D. Bond and V. Griffin. London: Kogan, 1987.

Hall, Douglas John. *Thinking the Faith: Christian Theology in a North American Context.* Minneapolis: Fortress Press, 1991.

Haughey, John C. "The Role of Prayer in Action/Reflection Groups." In *Tracing the Spirit: Communities, Social Action, and Theological Reflection.* New York: Paulist Press, 1993.

Holmes, Bob. "Following Jesus at a Distance: A Lenten Reflection on Discipleship." *The Mustard Seed* (Lent 1997): 5.

Infoplease.com. Countries Hosting Refugees, 2006. http://www.infoplease .com/ipa/A0931917.html (accessed September 15, 2008).

Johnson, Elizabeth A. *She Who Is: The Mystery of God in Feminist Theological Discourse.* New York: Crossroad, 1993.

————. "Redeeming the Name of Christ." In *Freeing Theology: The Essential of Theology in Feminist Perspective,* edited by Catherine Mowry LaCugna. San Francisco: Harper Collins, 1993.

Killen, Patricia O'Connell, and John de Beer. *The Art of Theological Reflection.* New York: Crossroad, 1994.

Kinast, Robert. *Let the Ministry Teach: A Handbook for Theological Reflection.* Maderia Beach, FL: Center for Theological Reflection, 1992.

————. *Making Faith-Sense: Theological Reflection in Everyday Life.* Collegeville, MN: Liturgical Press, 1999.

Komonchak, Joseph A., Mary Collins, and Dermot Lane, eds. *The New Dictionary of Theology.* Collegeville, MN: Liturgical Press, 1993. S.v. "Conversion" by James Walter; s.v. "Mercy" by Irene Nowell; s.v. "Ministry" by Thomas F. O'Meara; and s.v. "Sin" by William E. May.

Lacon, Dom Marc-Francois. "Conversion and Kingdom in the Synoptic Gospels." In *Conversion: Perspectives on Personal and Social Transformation,* edited by Walter E. Conn. New York: Paulist Press, 1978.

Leddy, Mary Jo. *At the Border Called Hope: Where Refugees Are Neighbours.* Toronto: Harper Collins, 1997.

Lonergan, Bernard J. F. *Method in Theology.* Toronto: University of Toronto Press, 1971.

————. "Theology in Its New Context." In *Conversion: Perspectives on Personal and Social Transformation,* edited by Walter E. Conn. New York: Paulist Press, 1987.

Macmurray, John. *Reason and Emotion*. London: Faber and Faber, 1936.

McDermott, Brian O. "The Relationship Among Authority, Leadership, and Spirituality in Ministry." In *Handbook of Spirituality for Ministers*, edited by Robert Wicks. New York: Paulist Press, 1995.

McDonnell, Maureen F. "The Tension Between the Professional and Vocational Dimensions of Spiritual Direction Ministry: A Contemporary Challenge Facing the Supervisor of Spiritual Directors." Doctor of Ministry thesis. The Toronto School of Theology at The University of Toronto, 2005.

McFague, Sallie. "Conversion: Life on the Edge of the Raft." *Interpretation: A Journal of Bible and Theology* 32, no. 3 (July 1978): 225–68.

Merton, Thomas. *Conjectures of a Guilty Bystander*. Toronto: Doubleday, 1968.

———. *Contemplation in a World of Action*. New York: Image Books, 1973.

———. *Contemplative Prayer*. New York: Image Books, 1990.

———. "Seeds of Contemplation." In *A Thomas Merton Reader*, edited and revised by Thomas P. McDonnell. Garden City, NY: Doubleday Image, 1974 [1962].

Mezirow, Jack. "Transformative Theory." Calgary, Alberta: Adult Education Research Conference, May 6–8, 1988.

———. *Transformative Dimensions of Adult Learning*. San Francisco: Jossey-Bass, 1991.

Miller, John P. *The Contemplative Practitioner: Meditation in Education and the Professions*. Toronto: OISE Press, 1994.

Moessner, Jeanne Stevenson. "A New Pastoral Paradigm and Practice." In *Women in Travail and Transition*, edited by Maxine Glaz and Jeanne Stevenson Moessner. Minneapolis: Fortress Press, 1991.

Nolan, Albert. "Contextual Theology: One Faith, Many Theologies." Address. Toronto: Regis College Publication, 1990.

O'Meara, Thomas Franklin. *Theology of Ministry*. New York: Paulist Press, 1999.

Palmer, Parker J. *To Know as We Are Known: Education as a Spiritual Journey*. San Francisco: Harper Collins, 1993.

Rahner, Karl. "Conversion." In *Encyclopedia of Theology: Concise Sacramentum Mundi*. New York: Seabury Press, 1975.

Rohr, Richard, and Joseph Martos. *The Wild Man's Journey: Reflections on Male Spirituality*. Cincinnati, OH: St. Anthony Messenger Press, 1992.

Saiving, Valerie. "The Human Situation: A Feminine View." In *Womanspirit Rising*, edited by Carol Christ and Judith Plaskow. San Francisco: Harper and Row, 1979.

Schillebeeckx, Edward. *Jesus.* New York: Seabury Press, 1979.

Schneiders, Sandra. "The Effects of Women's Experience on Their Spirituality." In *Women's Spirituality*, edited by Joann Wolski Conn. New York: Paulist Press, 1986.

————. *What is Theology? What Ever Happened to the One Right Answer?* Video. Monroe, MI: Sisters, Servants of the IHM, 1995.

Schon, Donald A. *Educating the Reflective Practitioner.* San Francisco: Jossey-Bass, 1987.

Schreiter, Robert. "A New Modernity: Living and Believing in an Unstable World." The 2005 Anthony Jordan Lectures, Newman Theological College, Edmonton, Alberta, March 18–19, 2005, pp. 1–3. http://www.mission-preciousblood.org/Docsfiles/schreiter_new_modernity.pdf (accessed March 15, 2006).

————. *Constructing Local Theologies.* Maryknoll, NY: Orbis Books, 2002.

————. "Plurality and Difference in an Unstable World." Lecture, January 24, 2004, Scarborough Mission Center, Toronto. http://www.mission-preciousblood.org/Docsfiles/schreiter-pluralityanddifference.doc (accessed March 10, 2006).

Schüssler Fiorenza, Elisabeth. *Discipleship of Equals: A Critical Ekklesia-ology of Liberation.* New York: Crossroad, 1993.

Sheehan, Mary Ellen. "Social Sciences and Theology: Mutually Necessary Conversation Partners." In *Festival Papers of IHM Theology Conference*, Monroe, MI, August 1995.

————. "Theological Reflection and Theory-Praxis Integration: An Experience with the Case Study Method." *Pastoral Studies* 3 (1984): 25–38.

Sobrino, Jon. *Christology at the Crossroads.* New York: Orbis Books, 1978.

————. "Samaritan Church and the Principle of Mercy." Paper presented as part of a symposium at Maryknoll School of Theology, Maryknoll, NY, October 1992.

————. *Spirituality of Liberation: Toward Political Holiness.* New York: Orbis Books, 1988.

————. *The Principle of Mercy: Taking the Crucified People from the Cross.* New York: Orbis Books, 1994.

Swan, Michael. "Safe Third Country Agreement Challenged by Churches," Canadian Christianity, 2008. http://www.canadianchristianity.com/nationalupdates/080828third.html (accessed September 16, 2008).

Tillich, Paul. *Systematic Theology: Reason and Revelation*. Vol. 1. Chicago: University of Chicago Press, 1973.

Tracy, David. "Theology and the Many Faces of Postmodernity." *Theology Today* 51, no. 1 (April 1994): 104–14.

United Nations High Commissioner for Refugees. Article 1, *The 1951 Convention Relating to the Status of Refugees*. Website: www.unhcr.org (accessed September 15, 2008).

———. *The State of the World's Refugees 2006*. http://www.unhcr.org/publ/PUBL/4444d3c220.html (accessed September 15, 2008).

Wainwright, Elaine. "The Gospel of Matthew." In *Searching the Scriptures: A Feminist Commentary*, edited by Elisabeth Schüssler Fiorenza. New York: Crossroad, 1994.

Whitehead, Evelyn Eaton, and James D. Whitehead. *Method in Ministry*. New York: Harper and Row, 1985.

Wolkam, Thomas. "State of the Right," *The Star*, 5 April, 1997, sec A.

Wolski Conn, Joann. *Spirituality and Personal Maturity*. New York: Paulist Press, 1989.

———. *Women's Spirituality: Resources for Christian Development*. New York: Paulist Press, 1996.

———. "Toward Spiritual Maturity." In *Freeing Theology: The Essentials of Theology in Feminist Perspective*, edited by Catherine Mowry LaCugna. San Francisco: Harper Collins, 1993.

Zanzig, Thomas. "The Process of Conversion and Implications for Ministry." In *The National Catholic Education Association: Proceedings of the 89th Annual Convention in St. Louis, Missouri, April 20–23, 1992*, Washington, DC: Chesapeake Audio/Video Comm., Inc., 1992.

INDEX